W9-AAT-028

Donated by

The Abreu Family

May 2020

Donated by
The Askew Family
May 2020

The Pedagogy

of the

21st Century

William A. Draves and Julie Coates

Published by LERN Books, a division of
Learning Resources Network (LERN)
P.O. Box 9
River Falls, Wisconsin 54022
U.S.A.

Phone: 800-678-5376 (US and Canada)
Email: *info@lern.org*
Web: *www.lern.org*

Manufactured in the United States of America

5   4   3   2   1

Library of Congress Cataloging in Publication Data
Draves, William A., 1949-

ISBN: 1-57722-040-4

"Information That Works!"

The Pedagogy of the 21st Century

Acknowledgments

The authors are indebted to Greg Marsello, Vice President for Organizational Development, Co-Founder of LERN, and the third member of our Senior Management Team, for his support of our work.

Numerous students, teachers, administrators and concerned members of the public have also contributed anecdotes, examples and assistance in data gathering, and we are thankful for their contributions.

We are indebted to those who came before us, such as Malcolm Knowles, Jerry Apps, and Peter Drucker. And we are in awe of those who come after us, Generation Y. We especially note the ongoing contributions of Jason Coates and Willie Draves to our work.

For production, thanks to Suzanne Kart and Stephanie Mason. Finally, we very much appreciate the Herculean efforts of our editors and proof readers, Nancy Hulverson and Nicole O'Shea. We, of course, take responsibility for the remaining grammatical and punctuation errors, as well as any instances of inconsistency. Such errors are the result of limits in time and resources, not our lack of desire for greater accuracy. We have focused our energies on the concepts of the book and ask the indulgence of the reader, as well as your reporting of any errors for future editions of the book.

Introduction:
Welcome to the 21st Century

It is an exciting century in which the marvelous inventions of the World Wide Web and the Internet have created a new economy leading to a different way of life for many people, including most people in the post-industrial nations such as Europe, Australia and New Zealand, Japan, Russia, Canada and the United States.

The new technology of the World Wide Web, along with its many offshoots, is transforming work, life and education. By 2020, some 75% of the ways in which we work, live and learn will be spent differently than they were in 2000. We know this because it happened once before, exactly 100 years ago, when we transitioned from the Agrarian Age into the Industrial Age between 1900 and 1920.

As we transition into the new economy and the new environment of the 21st century, the infrastructure and institutions of the former economy and century become obsolete. The new age simply demands a new kind of infrastructure, and institutions have to be transformed in order to remain relevant.[1]

Our educational system is one such critical element of the social infrastructure that has to be transformed. Our current educational system, which has served society so well for the past 100 years, is now obsolete. It cannot be fixed. The model is broken. But while our educational system cannot be fixed, it can and is being transformed into a more relevant educational system for the learners of the 21st century. Just as the rural one-room school was not bad, it simply became obsolete, unable to provide the kind and quality of education necessary for the Industrial Age of the last century. For the same reason, and in the same way, the factory model educational system of the Industrial Age is no longer relevant for the new economy, the Internet Age, of the 21st century.

There was nothing bad about the rural one-room schoolhouse. In fact, there were some very positive aspects to it, even a few superior features that ought to be resurrected and implemented again in education. The problem with the one-room schoolhouse was that work was changing and society was changing, and thus the needs of students in the last century were totally different than the needs of students in the Agrarian Age of the 19th century.

The educational system that is mainly in place now, the one we have had for the past 100 years, the one that is obsolete, is based on the factory. In fact, most all organizational structures have been based on the factory model for the past 100 years, including organizations from business and corporations to government to nonprofit organizations to associations, voluntary clubs, even sports teams and arguably churches.

The factory model, while serving the interests of the manufacturing sector quite well, is only partially related to the production of tangible goods. The key aspect of the factory model is that it is a model for human supervision, for designing how people function and act. So while you may work in an office or a college, you essentially work in a factory.

More importantly, our students learn in the factory setting of their educational institutions, and faculty and instructors teach not only in the factory setting, but teach in a way which is determined by the factory system.

But like the Industrial Age which produced it, the factory model of education in our post-industrial societies is collapsing. There is no one to blame. There is essentially nothing to be done, that can be done, that should be done, to save it. Instead, there is much to be done in transforming the educational system for the nations of the post-industrial world into a completely different educational system relevant to the needs of our current students, and those succeeding generations of students in the 21st century.

The mark of the factory on our educational institutions is pervasive, but here are a few examples:

- When you approach the typical high school, it looks just like a factory.
- When teachers take attendance and require attendance, those practices come from the factory model.

- When all students have to be on the same chapter, sometimes even the same page, of the text book at the same time, that is the factory model.
- When homework and coursework have due dates and penalties for being late, that is the factory model.
- When the tardy bell goes off, that is the factory model.
- When grades are assigned, they compare one student to another - another feature of the factory model.
- When time must be devoted and work must be done to pass a course, that is the factory model.

Most all educators not only take these features of our educational system for granted, they also believe in the value and worth of these features.

These features did have function, did have a purpose, in the last century. They indeed were worth believing in during the Industrial Age. As long as most students were headed to the factory, or the office, or to management, and most of the rest of the students were headed towards jobs or living situations which utilized the management structure of the pyramid, then the factory model was both functional and worth valuing.

But as we will see, your current students and all succeeding generations of students in this century, in post-industrial societies, are decidedly not headed to the factory, not even to the office, and will not and cannot be supervised under the pyramid structure, then the factory model is no longer relevant, no longer functional, and no longer worth believing in and valuing.[2]

This transition is happening now. All nine major predictions we stated in our turn-of-the-century work *"Nine Shift: Work, life and education in the 21st century,"* have come or are in the process of becoming true. When the book was first published, we as authors had to document, justify and prove the worth of our predictions. Ten years later, the onus of documentation, justification and proof has switched to those who do not see these shifts happening.[3]

Now, in the second decade of the century, is the time when the new era emerges. This is the decade when the old order collapses, and a new, never-before-seen infrastructure has to be created. A critical component of that societal infrastructure in post-industrial nations is a new educational system at the elementary, secondary and higher education levels.

Now is the time when we create the educational system for the

3

Internet Age of the 21st Century. By 2020 we will basically know almost all of the key elements and components of the new system. Your co-authors already know some of those components now, components which are the subject of this book.

It is an exciting time to be in education. It is a time when we can learn both from the wisdom and experience of our elders, and from the innate intuition and instincts of the young as they respond to their environment, their lives, their future. It is a time when our own knowledge and wisdom are of worth and value to our students, and a time when the sharing of our knowledge is ever more gratifying and rewarding. And it is a time when we each have the opportunity, whether we assume it or not, to be a 'player,' an active participant in the creation of this new unnamed and unformed educational system.

This century, like the last century, will be better than the previous one for most people. Most of your students will have a higher quality of life and better standard of living than we and you have had. That is good. That is the purpose of education. That is the goal to which we in education all aspire.

Our book written at the beginning of the century is called *Nine Shift: Work, life and education in the 21st century*. It has received positive, and sometimes rave, reviews from people all over the world. This book is based on our work for Nine Shift and specifically explores the necessity to transform our educational system between now and 2020. It is intended to be practical and to outline the framework of the new educational system of the 21st century. Most of its ideas and concepts can, should and will be implemented. A few of the ideas and concepts in this first edition of *The Pedagogy of the 21st Century* will be superseded in the coming years as our understanding of education in this century changes, the experience of learners in this century deepens, and learners and educators create new ways of learning and teaching. Thus we as co-authors envision this book to experience several revisions and editions as we head towards 2020. We do not know everything about how learning, teaching and education will be different in this century from the previous one, but we know enough to get started. As a young person of age ten today already needs to be preparing for her or his life in the year 2040, we also know we have to get started now in making education relevant to this century.

We begin this book with a review of our "Nine Shift" work, which establishes the fundamental changes going on, and the new economy, work, and way of life in the 21st century. Because education has always, in part, responded to the economic and social needs of society, one needs to understand the big picture in order to understand the pedagogy of the 21st century. We then go on to explore the implications of the Internet Age for learning, teaching and education.

While we have consciously used the word pedagogy, the art of teaching, to describe the emphasis of this work, we understand that andragogy, the art of learning, is far more important and determinant of the new structuring of our education system.[4]

This work is intended for anyone interested in learning, teaching or education, from students to teachers to prospective teachers to administrators to civic, business and community leaders. It is intended to be relevant for elementary, secondary, and higher education.

Welcome to the pedagogy of the 21st century.

Chapter 1.
Nine Shift: Work, life and education in the 21st century

Every once in awhile, a technology comes along that is so influential that it changes the way we live. Work, life and education are reorganized around the technology, and it defines a given age. Such is the case with both the automobile and the World Wide Web, which we will refer to by its more common name, the Internet.

Before proceeding with explaining our new research and thinking about how education must be, and is being, transformed, we have to summarize the economic changes which necessitate the transformation of education at this time. This chapter is a review of our earlier book *"Nine Shift: work, life and education in the 21st century."* It intentionally restates, in considerably condensed form, the underlying technological and economic changes that have created the new economic era of the Internet Age and the new conditions which require learning, teaching and education to be redesigned.

The Internet is the physical structure connecting computers all over the world, a structure created in the late 1960s by scientists, universities and the Department of Defense of the United States. The World Wide Web was begun in 1989 and completed around 1992 by British computer programmer Tim Berners Lee, now Sir Tim Berners Lee, when he was working for the nonprofit organization CERN in Switzerland. The World Wide Web is the common language, including the "http://" and hypertext which allows everyone to communicate using the Internet. While understanding the difference between the Internet and the World Wide Web, for simplicity sake we will refer to this technology as simply the Internet.

There are more important inventions, to be sure. Electricity and the printing press are two. But their influences span the centuries and do not define a particular age. Electricity has been equally valuable in the 19th, 20th and 21st centuries. The printing press has played a critical role in society for the past 500 years.

There are also many inventions that have become universal, yet have not substantially changed how we work or live. Movies, television, radio and airplanes are a few examples. The airplane, for instance, changed how we travel, but has not fundamentally changed how we shop, where we live or the basic nature of our jobs.

A transformative technology changes how we live. Here's how it happens.

- The technology changes the economy, including the means of production, how we build things, buy things and sell things.
- The new economy then changes the job structure, including what jobs are needed, valued and available.
- The new job structure then changes the work place, and how we work.
- How we work and earn a living are so central to life that home and family are impacted.
- The new living situation then determines the nature of our local community.
- The new economy, new job structure, and nature of work also determine how we prepare young people for the workplace, and so education and schools are redesigned.
- Finally, all of the above changes lead to a new set of values and attitudes.

The changes are not totally sequential. Many of them occur concurrently. And the changes are not completed all at once. They may take several decades to play themselves out. But all in all, this is how it happens.

One hundred years ago the technology of the automobile changed life.[1] Here's how the sequence of change played out in the 20th century.

- The automobile created a mass demand for goods, and the auto's cousin the tractor created a decrease in the number of farmers needed for the production of food. This led to a significant increase in the output of factories and mass production of goods.
- The increase in factory output led to a dramatic increase in factory and office jobs, and the decline of farm jobs.

- The factory and office led to the organization chart and the behavioral norms and expectations of the factory and office. A few examples include the 40-hour work week, first, second and third shifts, starting work at a precise time, hourly wages, and supervision and middle management.
- The industrialized work situation led to greater family mobility, the nuclear family and the decline of the extended family.
- The nuclear family led to suburbs.
- The factory and office led to mandated universal high school education, the consolidation of schools, age-grades, and schools that look and function like offices and factories.
- New values and attitudes set in. They include shopping on Sunday, driving on Sunday, moving as a positive sign of upward mobility, and much more.

The 20th century is widely called the "Industrial Age" because industry jobs (factory and office) rose to constitute half of all the jobs in the economy during the century. The Industrial Age is not the same as the Industrial Revolution, which took place in the early 1800s. The factory was created in the Industrial Revolution. But factory jobs did not surpass farm jobs until the 20th century, the Industrial Age. In 1900 close to half of all Americans lived on farms. By 1920 factory employment had surpassed farm employment, which continued to decline as a percentage of workers.[2]

The same scenario is playing out now with the Internet, impacting work, life and education changes once again. Here's how it is playing out in the 21st century.

- The Internet has created a different kind of economy, one in which mass customization is possible, information and knowledge are critical, distance is no longer a barrier (and sometimes is an advantage), intangibles such as speed, design and customer service rise in importance, and technology takes over an ever-growing number of routine tasks for people.
- At the same time, the resulting technology allows manufactured goods to be produced by fewer factory workers, as well as in countries where labor is less expensive, causing a huge decline in the number of people employed in manufacturing.
- The technology creates knowledge jobs, those jobs which utilize a person's thinking skills to a high degree. Knowledge jobs in this century are the most valuable jobs. Knowledge workers earn more than workers in other sectors. Knowledge workers also

9

create an average of four additional local jobs in the community.
* Knowledge workers grow in number, and find that they not only can do their work at home, but that they can do it better from home.
* With a workforce now primarily working from home, companies find that not only are physical offices a liability, but that intranets can accomplish what the office used to do, and the intranets can do it better.
* With people working from home, they become linked to each other in relatively small business units that are more flexible and efficient than in large departmental structures. Organizations are thus reconfigured into networks instead of the pyramid of the organization chart.
* With time being the principle resource of a knowledge worker, time becomes far more valuable. Consequently people desire shops, stores, clubs and centers close to home. Thus communities become much denser.
* Commuting becomes unnecessary and driving wastes too much time, so knowledge workers switch to trains and light rail for transportation, able to work while they are traveling.
* Social structures, government policy, federal and state safety nets are all redesigned around the new economic reality of the 21st century.
* To prepare young people for this new work environment, schools and colleges become web-based, just like the business organizations in which students will work.

The economy of the Agrarian Age was based on the farmer. The economy of the Industrial Age of the 20th century was based on the factory worker. The new economy of the 21st century for post-industrial nations depends upon, revolves around, and is driven by knowledge workers.

In the last century, factory jobs were prized because every factory worker created four additional local jobs in the community. Factory goods were sold outside of the community, so money came into the community from other communities, states, even other nations, and that money created an average of four additional jobs for every factory worker. This is why so many communities had industrial parks in the last century, because recruiting factories to one's town meant significant additional local employment. In this century, knowledge workers are the most important work sector, because each knowledge worker creates an average of four additional jobs in the local community. Again, the work or intangible output of a knowledge worker is used outside of the community, in other states, and in other nations, and again money comes in to the local community from that knowledge job, once again creating additional local jobs.

Economists tell us that communities grow and prosper when outside money comes into that community. When the grocery store worker buys clothes, and the clothing store worker buys groceries, not as much economic growth is achieved because local existing dollars are just moving back and forth in the community. When a knowledge worker buys groceries and clothes, however, she or he uses money that came in from outside of the community, and these new non-local dollars create more economic activity. So we will need welders and retailers and electricians in this century, but a community's economic prosperity will be dependent on how many knowledge workers it has, bringing in new outside money into the community with which to pay welders, electricians and retailers.

The concept and term knowledge work and knowledge worker was created by the business and management guru Peter F. Drucker. Drucker accurately predicted and explained how and why knowledge workers are emerging and changing the nature of business organizations. He wrote, "Both in its speed and its impact, the Information Revolution uncannily resembles its two predecessors within the past two hundred years, the First Industrial Revolution of the later eighteenth and early nineteenth centuries, and the Second Industrial Revolution of the late nineteenth century." Drucker predicted, "The Next Society will be a knowledge society. Knowledge will be its key resource, and knowledge workers will be the dominant group in its work force."[3]

Knowledge workers will become from 25% to 50% of workers in society, but more importantly, they become the most valued work sector in the economy, what Drucker called the "dominant" sector. Knowledge workers produce intangible goods as opposed to tangible goods, which the manufacturing sector produces. Some examples of intangible goods are data analysis, financial services, consulting, virtual models, training, and management.

Because the economy becomes more specialized, segmented and niched, knowledge workers are very specialized and work in very segmented and niched occupations and professions. They say in the last century there were dozens of jobs for millions of people and in this century there are millions of jobs for dozens of people.

Knowledge workers generally need a four-year college degree for at least two reasons. One reason is that the changing nature of the knowledge economy means that it is very difficult to prepare a student for a specific job. Another reason is that knowledge workers usually require the higher level of learning and knowledge that comes from a four-year college or university course of study.

We know, backed by statistics but also history, that knowledge workers are succeeding factory workers as the most valuable work sector.

In 1900, at the beginning of the last century, farm workers were 50% of those employed in society. Then as the economic impact of the automobile took effect, the percentage of people employed in farming declined and the percentage of factory workers increased. Between 1910 and 1920 the percentage of workers in factory jobs surpassed the percentage of workers who were farmers, and we went from the Agrarian Age into the Industrial Age. The percentage of workers in factory jobs rose to an average of 35% of employees, and peaked at 50%.

In 2000, at the beginning of this century, factory workers were the dominant work sector. Then as the economic impact of the Internet took effect, the percentage of people employed in factories declined and the percentage of knowledge workers increased. As Drucker explained, "The blue-collar worker in manufacturing industry and his union are going the way of the farmer. The newly emerging dominant group is 'knowledge workers'."[4] Between 2010 and 2020 the percentage of knowledge workers will surpass the percentage of workers who are factory workers, and we will officially leave the Industrial Age and enter the Internet Age.

Because the technology of the Internet is so powerful, just like the technology of the automobile was, no one or no entity can reverse the trend. Like it did 100 years ago, life has to change again in accordance with the requirements of the Internet Age.

Employment determines where we live, how we live, what we are able to do in much of our non-work time, and much more. Just as it was nigh impossible for most people to work in a factory and then return home at night to the family farm, so it is nigh impossible for most people today to work as knowledge workers and then return at night to a life embedded in the Industrial Age.

Suburbs, commuting, malls, two-week vacations and television were just some of the products of life in the Industrial Age. In the same way, as we move into the Internet Age, so life and education get redesigned for this new way of life. This is a nine shift.

Thus, in just twenty years, from 2000 to 2020, some 75% of our lives is changing. We know this because it happened once before. Between 1900 and 1920 life changed as we moved from the Agrarian Age into the Industrial Age.

The term "nine shift" is used to describe the great changes taking place in our lives right now. What we are experiencing in how we use our time, and how we experience life derives from the phenomenon that nine hours in your day will be spent differently in 2020 than they were spent in 2000.

There are 24 hours in a day. We have no real discretion with roughly 12 of those hours. We need to eat, sleep and do a few other necessary chores in order to maintain our existence. That leaves approximately 12 hours a day where we, as individuals, do have some discretion. That includes work time, play time and family time.

Of those 12 hours, about 75%, or 9 hours, will be spent differently a few years from now than they were spent just a few years ago. Not everything will change, but 75% of life is in the process of changing right now. That same kind of change occurred between 1900 and 1920 as well. Frederick Allen called it "the big change" in his 1952 book by the same title.[5] We call it a nine shift.

By 1920, almost all of the major inventions of the century had seen the light of day. They included radio, movies, airplanes, the gasoline engine, and more. About the only device to have a major impact on us that had not yet been invented was the television. Yet even there, the visual language for television was established by 1920, according to television and communications expert Kathleen McMonigal.[6]

More importantly, by 1920 almost all of the major aspects of 20th century life had emerged. They include suburbs, commuting, offices, factories, the National Football League, women's right to vote, and possibly most importantly, the ubiquitous organization chart or pyramid.

In terms of education, by 1920 most of the features of education of the last century had been devised, including the factory school model, the Carnegie Unit measurement of learning, community colleges, and more. The rural one-room schoolhouse was in decline. Normal schools, those post-secondary institutions that prepared people to become one-room schoolhouse teachers, were being redesigned to become teacher colleges and then state universities.

In our earlier work we were alone in predicting nine major changes would take place in society. We now have clear evidence that all nine shifts are coming true. The nine shifts.

Shift One. People work at home.

Commuting to an office becomes a rarity, a thing of the past. A significant part of the workforce works from home or from one or more other chosen locations instead of commuting to a central office. People who work from home are 25% more productive than people who work in an office. They often work longer than office workers, yet have more free time for their families and leisure time. People who work from home are less stressed, healthier, safer and more connected to their local communities and to their children and families.

People who work from home are able to work during their peak productivity hours. Peak productivity time, like peak learning time for students, is not the same for every person. Some 50% of people are most productive in the morning, and 25% of people are most productive in the afternoon. But 20% of people are most productive in the evening, well after most offices have closed, and some 6% of people are most productive overnight (the percentages equal 101% due to rounding). One consequence of this is that people who work from home have a greater sense of the value of time, the most important resource for knowledge workers.

Since we made this prediction, the number of teleworkers has steadily increased, and the percentage of workers engaged in working from home has also steadily increased. Working from home will soon become the norm for employees with any business organization, including corporations, government and education.[7]

Shift Two. Intranets replace offices.

As offices decline, they are replaced by Intranets. Intranets are password-protected web sites designed specifically for the communication, work and needs of people working in a given company, business or organization.

The job descriptions of people who work from home change from activities or inputs to outcomes and results. As a result, people working from home can be supervised better from a distance than office workers are supervised face-to-face.

Intranets also allow organizations to recruit the best people, no matter where they live. Knowledge organizations require human resources with very specialized skills, and organizations compete best when they have the best people. Intranets allow organizations to maximize their human resources, and Intranets allow workers to communicate, be supervised, and get work done in a flexible manner that optimizes the quality of both work and leisure time for teleworkers.

Shift Three. Networks replace pyramids.
The basic organizational structure of work in the last century, the organization chart or pyramid, is in steep decline. It is being replaced by a superior organizational structure, the network.[8]

The pyramid or organization chart is dysfunctional for the 21st century in several ways. The pyramid concentrates knowledge at the top, whereas in this century everyone in the organization needs access to all of the information in the organization in order to maximize their performance and solving of problems. Organizations with a pyramid structure have to waste some of their best people in supervisory positions, supervising the work of others instead of producing income or cost savings themselves. Organizations with a pyramid structure have interlocking and interdependent units or departments, meaning that units or departments are often limited in their ability to get tasks done by a dependency on another unit or department. And of course the pyramid creates a hierarchical reward structure so that only a few chosen people and positions are valued most highly, while most people and positions are valued less with the opportunity for advancement only at the expense and comparison of others in the organization. The pyramid inherently compares people to other people within the organization, assigning a worker's value based on the value of others rather than on one's own achievements, outcomes and results independent of the value of any other person in the organization.

For these reasons, the pyramid is collapsing while the network is emerging as the organizational structure of the 21st century. In their book *The Centerless Corporation*, Bruce A. Pasternack and Albert S. Viscio described the network as being composed of business units. Each business unit has a central function or purpose, and each business unit has the resources necessary to do its job. A business unit might be one or two people, or as many as twenty or more.[9]

People in a business unit might, and often do, work with each from a distance. People in different business units communicate with each other based on each other's need for information, not based on any pyramid-based permission or information allocation system. People have access to people and information whenever and however they wish or need to get their jobs done.

Someone working at IBM described to us the transition in communication from a pyramid structure to a network in his company this way. "Before, if I emailed the vice president of another division, I would have been fired. Now if email the vice president of another division and she does not respond, she gets fired."

Advancement for individuals is no longer dependent on rising above someone else in the organization. Individual reward is based on value to the organization instead of an artificial comparison to someone else or another position in the organization.

For the leadership of the organization, the network structure also allows the organization to be more flexible, adaptable, and changing according to the changing circumstances of the business environment.

Shift Four. Trains replace cars.

The automobile, the dominant mode of transportation in the last century, is losing its dominance and becoming peripheral and supplemental mode of transportation. Trains and light rail are becoming the dominant modes of transportation.[10]

There are three major reasons why trains are replacing cars.

1. *One cannot work and drive at the same time.*

On a train or light rail, one can work and travel at the same time. Time is so valuable to knowledge workers they cannot afford to waste two to three hours a day driving, some 25% of their productive time. Economically, workers and businesses simply cannot compete successfully wasting 25% of their productive time.

2. *Cars are destroying the environment.*

For Generation Y, the car is responsible for an unacceptably high proportion of pollution, global warming, killing of wildlife, water pollution, and energy consumption. When the related auto lifestyle of suburbs, lawns, offices, malls, and sprawl are included, the cost of automobiles for the environment simply outweighs their value to this generation.

Trains and light rail make substantially less environmental impact to the point where trains and light rail are sustainable environmentally. While autos in the United States require asphalt and paving land equivalent to the size of Georgia, train tracks take up substantially less space with less pollution. While trucks and cars get between 10 and 50 miles per gallon, a freight train can transport one ton of material 454 miles on a single gallon of gasoline at one-third the cost of truck travel.

3. *Cars kill too many people.*

Cars kill over one million people a year worldwide. Despite laws, safety classes, and improvements in cars, the death statistics have not declined much. Many of these deaths are simply unavoidable, according to Malcolm Gladwell, who writes, "Every two miles, the average driver makes four hundred observations, forty decisions, and one mistake. Once every five hundred miles, one of those mistakes leads to a near collision, and once every sixty-one thousand miles one of those mistakes leads to a crash."[11]

For young people, cars are the leading cause of death. As the large Baby Boomer generation ages, cars become an ever-more-deadly way of travel.[12]

The cost to society is just too great in terms of lost talent and the loss on a human and family level. Like airplanes, trains have a safety record that can save thousands of lives a year, providing safe transportation.

There are many other reasons why trains and light rail are replacing cars, of course. Some of them are that trains are faster than cars, cars take up space in storage, cars require insurance, there is no drunk driving on a train, and many more.

Shift Five. Dense neighborhoods replace suburbs.

Suburbs and suburban sprawl are coming to a halt, and then suburbs recede and even become destroyed as they become financially valueless. Towns and cities already are being reformulated around dense communities composed of shops, stores and homes within walking distance of a light rail or train station.[13]

Shift Six. New social infrastructures evolve.

The increasing inequality in wealth between the rich and the rest of society comes to a halt. The unsustainable inequality in wealth of 100 years came to a halt and then the income gap closed as necessary social reforms took place to sustain the growing middle class of the last century. For the very same reason, the inequality of wealth in society today is addressed, and a variety of social reforms are implemented to create a new infrastructure for the general good of everyone in society, restoring more of a balance in income distribution.

Shift Seven. Cheating Becomes Collaboration.
New values, work ethics and behavior of the 21st century take over. For example, taking less time to learn or accomplish something becomes more valuable than devoting more time to the task. Working in teams becomes more valued than working independently. Hacking becomes a valued skill, seen as a way to find out how something works. Collaborative learning is encouraged and taught.

Shift Eight. Half of all learning is online.
The traditional classroom rapidly becomes obsolete. Half of all learning is done online overall in education, changing the nature of how we learn and how we teach. Hybrid or web-enhanced learning that incorporates both online learning and face-to-face learning becomes almost universal and commonplace, replacing the traditional face-to-face learning with a superior mode of learning.

Shift Nine. Education becomes web-based.
Brick and mortar schools and colleges of the past century are outdated. All education becomes web-based, providing a better education for both young people and adults.

In summary, learning, teaching and how education is structured and delivered are transformed as a result and consequence of the transition from the Industrial Age to the Internet Age. As we now explore the implications for learning, teaching and administering schools and colleges, all of the concepts, practices and strategies relate in some part or all to the economic and lifestyle requirements of the 21st century. *The Pedagogy of the 21st Century* responds to the new needs of our students in preparing them for work and life in the Internet Age.

Section I.
Learning, Teaching and Schools

Just like the one-room school became obsolete as we transitioned from the Agrarian Age into the Industrial Age one hundred years ago, so the factory model for the school and college of the 20th century is now obsolete as we transition from the Industrial Age into the Internet Age of the 21st century.

The critical shift is that education becomes personalized. Instead of treating students the same, we treat each learner differently. There are both economic and pedagogical reasons for doing this. The existing factory model of education is simply not able to address the economic or pedagogical needs of students in preparing them to become knowledge workers in the Internet Age. Based on the factory model, our schools and colleges are broken. They cannot be fixed. However, they can, and will, be transformed.

While the one-room school model took several decades of decline before it disappeared for all practical purposes in industrial society, the factory school model was constructed, established and recognized as superior by around 1920. And by 2020 we should have a pretty good idea what the 21st century school and college will look like.

In this section we outline what we know already about the mission of schools and colleges, the curriculum, the role of the teacher, how assessment will be done, how grading will change, how the shift from cars to trains will impact education, and some critical financial considerations in budgeting for schools and colleges in this century.

In order to function successfully as knowledge workers, our youth need to acquire a different set of behaviors, values, attitudes, work habits and learning styles than that required for success in the factory and office environment of the Industrial Age of the last century. In this section we also build on our earlier work and offer our first set of 21 pedagogical concepts for this century. It is these learning and pedagogical concepts and practices which the 21st century school and college must foster, and which determines the structure and characteristics of the 21st century educational system.

Chapter 2.
The Mission of Education:
Only One Thing Matters

In the school, college and university of the 21st century, only one thing matters. That "thing" is learning and knowledge.

Today, the factory model of schools and colleges that worked so well in the industrial age of the last century no longer works. As Bill Gates noted in 2005, "America's high schools are obsolete. By obsolete, I don't just mean that they're broken, flawed or underfunded, though a case could be made for every one of those points. By obsolete, I mean our high schools even when they're working as designed cannot teach all our students what they need to know today." The same can be said for our elementary schools as well as our colleges and universities. In transforming our schools and colleges and creating a new educational model for this century, we start with revising the mission of schools and colleges.

In the knowledge economy of this century, the only thing that students must absolutely take away from their education is learning and knowledge. They can have school spirit, but they do not need it. They can enjoy a football game, but they do not need it. They ought to be physically fit, but that is not the sole responsibility nor mission of the school.

To gain knowledge and learning, there are, of course, some fundamental tools necessary. Every student needs a computer and wireless 24-hour access to the Internet. Students need teachers, as every study concludes that the teacher is the most critical component in a person's education.

The mission of K-12 schools is no longer to graduate students from high school. That was the mission of the last century, to prepare students for the Industrial Age. The 21st century mission of K-12 schools is to prepare students to be accepted and to graduate from a four-year higher education institution. The mission of K-12 schools is to send, with few exceptions due to mental abilities, every one of its graduates on to a four-year higher education. The Memphis, Tennessee public school system gets it right with its motto "Every child. Every day. College bound." This school system, which has one of the most challenging tasks of all, to educate low income and minority children, is insistent about its goal, so that almost every half hour on the district's radio station, one can hear the motto repeated, reinforcing the notion among students, parents, faculty and citizenry.

In the last century it was enough- - it was the goal- - of K-12 education for every student to have a high school degree. In this century, that is no longer enough. In the last century, a high school degree was enough for a good middle-class job in a factory, office, store or service sector organization. Now students need to graduate not only from high school, but also from higher education with a four-year undergraduate degree.

That is one reason why teacher incentives are beginning to shift to measuring teacher success by how many students are successful in their academic programs.

The near term mission of colleges and universities is to graduate one half of all children in society with four-year undergraduate degrees. This is not one half of college students, but one half of all children in society. By the end of the 21st century, post-industrial societies may need almost all of their children to be college graduates, just like near the end of the 20th century we needed almost all of our children to be high school graduates.

In order to have a sufficiently skilled workforce for the knowledge economy of the 21st century, we simply need 50% of our youth to have four-year undergraduate degrees. We need some of them, more than in the past, to have graduate degrees. We need most of them to also gain certificates in one or more work related skill sets. But we absolutely must have half of our children with four-year, not two-year, undergraduate degrees. Without that, we do not have enough skilled knowledge workers and professionals to maintain a viable and prosperous post-industrial economy, with a sufficient standard of living for its citizens, and adequate contributions to pension, retirement, social security and medical benefits for retired citizens.

For almost all four-year institutions, the mission today is just the opposite- - to keep out students and graduate fewer, not more students. Today colleges and universities are ranked not by how many students they graduate, but by how many they turn away. The best colleges and universities, so they say, are those that turn away the most students.

As a result we have an entire higher educational system whose motive and money come from restricting, not broadening, access to higher education.

There are some things schools should not have. Schools should not have school buses. They should not have as many buildings and as much physical space as they now have, constantly building the McMansions of the education world.

What we have now in the factory school model is a muddled expanse of activities not focused on the core mission of the school.[1] There are activities unrelated to learning and knowledge, such as mowing the lawn, and the football team. And there are expenses used by a few but paid for by everyone, to the exclusion of expenses for other students. For example, a school might have music and drama, but not Japanese or debate.

Schools should be more of a part of the community. Gymnasiums and swimming pools should be operated by the community, not the school. But if the gym or pool is already located at the school, then the community should use the school's gym and swimming pool whenever the students do not. Every school system should have a community education program, providing classes to adults in the community. However that does not mean that school funds should pay for these activities.

We like football (both futbol and American football), music, drama, school lunches, exercise weight rooms, theaters, marching bands, school trips to Washington DC, debate teams, and more. But unless it is integrally tied to learning and knowledge, and part of a student's individual learning contract, it is not the mission of the school.

Given the huge challenge, the limited resources, the number of hours in a day, and the essential, fundamental, and critical need for half of our nation's youth to have four-year undergraduate degrees, other important, nice, charitable and good-hearted activities are secondary.[2]

Once we have 50% of our nation's children with four-year under-graduate degrees, then schools and colleges can undertake other activities. Until then, schools and colleges must focus on the critical objective of education, learning and knowledge.[3]

Chapter 3.
Curriculum in the 21st Century: Does content matter?

One of the current and ongoing debates among all those concerned with education - -not just teachers, but parents, the media, government officials, business leaders, religious leaders, and other leaders, and students themselves - - is about what students should be learning. For some, the answers seem obvious. Students should master the basics, just as they have always done, and then move into more specialized content areas as they mature. This is where things become unclear: in the 21st century, what content matters? Does content matter at all? That is, is there a substantive foundation of content that every student should know in order to survive and prosper in a post-industrial society? And at this point, so early in the century, can adults who are "immigrants" and not "natives" to the 21st century determine what those content areas are?

Perhaps we can agree on reading, writing and arithmetic, or perhaps even that traditional core can be called into question, given online calculators, spell checkers and instant audio translations of the written word. There is a plethora of subjects, from Mandarin Chinese to ballroom dance manners, all having advocates, and all being taught in some but not all schools. The big question is "what is important and why?" What are the basic skills of the 21st century?

Universities from medieval times through to the 20th century taught the quadrivium, a set of four core subjects every student learned. The quadrivium consisted of arithmetic, geometry, music, and astronomy. These followed the preparatory work of the trivium made up of grammar, logic (or dialectic, as it was called at the times), and rhetoric (an art of using language as a means to entertain or persuade). These core areas formed the basis of a solid education because they were seen as bodies of knowledge necessary to achieve distinction of thought and scholarly success. Further, it was the role of universities to educate youth who would become the innovators, the thinkers, the philosophers, and the scientists who would guide the development of civilization and society to higher levels of knowledge and understanding.

Existing Curriculum Model

The existing curriculum model also has a set of core subjects, with teachers assigned to teach each subject. Students are tested on these core subjects to assure that they have mastered the basic skills necessary to be productive citizens and workers. There are a number of problems with the existing curriculum model.

Disagreement over ideal core subjects.

There is no consensus on what should comprise the ideal core subject matter right now, and there is no procedure or process to determine what should be offered.

There are excellent arguments for just about any subject. Music, for example, was essential to the quadrivium but is not essential for all students now. The argument has been made for adding cooking classes as cooking is central to good health, and good health to good learning. The argument has been made for the return of Latin. As Chinese is the language of some 25% of the world's population, there is an argument that students should learn Chinese. And on and on.

There is no end to the "wish list" for core subjects, depending on whom one talks to. This not only makes for a lack of consensus, but also strains the curriculum at the edges as schools have added to the tasks of teachers over the years.

One cannot predict future core or essential knowledge sets.

At this time we simply do not know what the essential knowledge sets will be for the Information Age and the rest of the 21st century. We know what was essential for the Agrarian Age of the 19th century. We have a pretty good idea what worked as the core subjects for the Industrial Age of the 20th century.

But right now we cannot predict what a given student will need to know in 2050. Our best guess is that each individual will want and need to know something different.

Motivation or enthusiasm inhibited.
Not every student wants to learn the same subject at the same time. This results in diminishing an individual's motivation and enthusiasm for learning, which does not help the person learn. It may also discourage self-directed learning, the inherent desire of each individual to learn what she or he wants to learn.

Skill and knowledge sets limited.
A limited curriculum leads to a limited skill and knowledge set. It may prepare everyone in a given set of knowledge skills, but it is not able to prepare some individuals in each of a wide variety of knowledge and skill sets which economists indicate are needed in a knowledge society. In past societies, where there were fewer occupations and thus fewer skill and knowledge sets needed, a limited curriculum can arguably be said to have worked. In a knowledge society, with new skill and knowledge sets being created on an ongoing basis, a limited curriculum can arguably be said to be out of date.

Self directed learning discouraged.
Self-directed learning is the desire and act of setting one's own learning goals. Some educators such as Malcolm Knowles contend the desire for self-directed learning is inherent in each individual. Self-directed learning contrasts with other directed learning, in which a teacher, school or other outside agent determines what someone learns. In the workplace of the 21st century, it is likely that more self-directed learning will be required, especially as individuals with increasingly divergent jobs and tasks have to rely on their own judgments for what learning is needed next. At the same time we see the growing need for more self-directed learning, we find employers telling us that young people entering the workplace need more direction, more specificity regarding work tasks, and more structure. It is not unreasonable to think that much of this approach to work and learning derives from the profound focus on a limited curriculum and rigorous testing which determines whether a student moves forward or not. Creativity, critical thinking, and self-direction are not the most highly regarded values in contemporary classrooms.

Individual talents not enhanced.

Limited core subject areas do not identify, enhance or maximize the student's individual talents and abilities. In the last century, we wanted a given benchmark or standard for all students. In this century, it is less clear whether we need every person to have the same amount of knowledge in each area, or whether society is actually served better by education that identifies, enhances and maximizes a person's individual and possibly distinct talents and abilities.

The result is that limited core subjects and same curriculum for all are no longer functional. In addition to what students should study, there is the issue of how students should study. We know that different individuals have different learning styles. We know individual students learn differently, and that different modes of delivery and teaching styles can enhance each student's learning. Schools need to create and make available different learning resources and design individual paths of learning. When we add the issue of learning styles to a limited core subject curriculum, it appears obvious that the 20th century core curriculum is obsolete for the 21st century.

Flexible Learning Situations

The U.K. instituted a new policy asking teachers to spend 25% of student time in flexible individually tailored learning situations a few years ago. Educators in the Qualifications and Curriculum Authority of the UK government appeared to be of two minds about the issue of essential curriculum.

"The head of the Qualifications and Curriculum Authority, Dr Ken Boston, insisted, the curriculum will still contain the essentials: grammar, Shakespeare, the British Empire and algebra. But Dr Boston also stated, quite unequivocally, that 'the traditional approach to covering the syllabus has been exhausted, it has delivered all it can, it will work no more.'

"The QCA's director of curriculum Mick Waters responds: 'Ann Boleyn will still be be-headed, Trafalgar will still have taken place in 1805, the Pennines will still be the backbone of England, acid will still turn litmus paper red and Romeo will still love Juliet.

These are things that have stood the test of time - they are things that our children need to know along with many others.'"[1]

BBC Education writer Mike Baker then went on to speculate on whether the "essential curriculum" side of the argument was serious, or whether UK education authorities were simply trying to introduce a radically new concept in education without disturbing too much the adult population, reassuring them that "Ann Boleyn will still be be-headed."

While acid turning litmus paper red and Romeo still loving Juliet are also part of the essential or traditional curriculum for students in the United States, one can reasonably debate and discuss what knowledge students in the Internet Age of the 21st century need to know to be successful and prosperous knowledge workers and citizens in the years ahead.

Process-oriented learning

Canadian educator Harold Jarche writes, "Our institutions have failed to foster the love of learning, and do not motivate students to learn for themselves – in many cases it's the opposite. I believe that the main cause of this is the continuing focus on subject-based curriculum. We do not live our lives in subject areas, and no workplace is subject-based, but almost all of our curricula are stuffed into category silos." [2] Jarche cites Peter Drucker's thoughts that "Delivering literacy — even on the high level appropriate to a knowledge society — will be an easier task than giving students the capacity and the knowledge to keep on learning, and the desire to do it. No school system has yet tackled that job. There is an old Latin tag: Non schola sed vita discimus (We don't learn for school but for life). But neither teacher nor student has ever taken it seriously."

Tan and Lim Ai Ming favor the separation of content (subject and disciplines) and process (learning and problem solving), stating "the retention of subjects or disciplines is an unnecessary obstacle to students' learning." Their paper is summarized by Jarche around these premises:
- Learning should be based on problems, not subjects.
- Subjects stress content rather than process.
- Individual learning is authentic [and group work may hinder this learning].
- When the teacher is also the assessor, then the power to fail students may be detrimental to self-directed learning.
- Teachers as content experts (such as at a university) may be detrimental to self-directed learning.
- Scheduled class times, as in any regulated school, are not

supportive of problem-based learning.[3]

David Warlick says that the web has so greatly increased the amount of available information that no one can master any content field any more.[4]

Jarche proposes eliminating content and replacing it with learning about learning, such as acquiring skills in particular technologies, processes, and learning techniques. He writes, "What would a curriculum look like if you eliminated any specific content and any reference to particular technologies and instead focused on universal cognitive processes?" Many varieties of this "curriculum" could be created, using various content areas or communication technologies. I imagine a curriculum that is open to teachers' expertise and learners' needs, based on processes like:

- Critical thinking
- Problem solving, individually and as part of a group
- Narrative development
- Media analysis & critique
- Self-expression, etc.

What would be different about this more basic curriculum is that learners would be able to choose how they would learn these process skills and how they would show mastery. Self-expression could be shown through writing, blogging, art or mechanics. This approach would also free up a whole bunch of teachers in administrative curriculum development positions.

In another post titled "First we kill the curriculum," Jarche maintains: "Our education system needs to drop the whole notion of subjects and content mastery and move to process-oriented learning. The subject matter should be something of interest to the learner or something a teacher, with passion, is motivated to teach. The subject does not matter; it's just grist for the cognitive mill.

"Discussing 'what' subjects we should teach is the 21st Century equivalent of determining how many angels can dance on the head of a pin. The answer is infinite. The real debate in education is whether we need linear, book-oriented curriculum at all."

Enthusiasm for learning

In a story on the new UK curriculum approach, the National Union of Teachers general secretary, Steve Sinnott, stated, "Only one thing matters. Does the curriculum help maintain youngsters' enthusiasm for learning?"

Sinnott put the apostrophe after the wrong letter but otherwise gets it right. He then says, "Cooking, Shakespeare and Mandarin are all important but at the moment they look like ministers' bright ideas rather than part of a coherent curriculum that will enthuse teachers and youngsters alike."[5]

Individually-tailored curricula

Revising the teachers' union comment just slightly, we arrive at the 21st century approach to curriculum. Only one thing matters. Does the curriculum help maintain a youngster's enthusiasm for learning?

If we continue to see "curriculum" as a given set for more than one student, we are left hopelessly behind in the factory mode of education, with "one size fits all" obsolescence.

One curriculum cannot maintain all youngsters' enthusiasm for learning. And in this century, maintaining a person's enthusiasm for learning is more important than content. But if we see curriculum as individually-tailored to each student, then we can achieve both goals of maintaining one's enthusiasm for learning and at the same time content mastery and achievement. As long as a student is learning something, anything, then that student and that school are doing their jobs.

We suggest that the curriculum in the 21st century will consist of around 10,000 subjects. Essentially, any student can learn anything.

The outstanding adult education professor Leonard Nadler of The George Washington University taught that in the 1970s, Japanese auto companies paid for their workers to take classes in origami, the traditional Japanese art of paper folding in which paper dolls, paper birds, paper flowers and other objects are created. The reason the employers allowed, encouraged and paid for this leisure craft was that they understood, according to Professor Nadler, that when it came time to learn a new technique on the auto assembly line that the workers would learn that new work technique more quickly and better as a result of their continued learning in other subjects.

Does that mean that an eight-year-old could spend all of his or her time learning rap music and rap lyrics and that would suffice?[6] Maybe. Or do only the Battle of Trafalgar and Gettysburg prepare students for the next level of learning? If the only thing a student learned was rap music and rap lyrics, then the new criteria of constant learning would not be met. What we know about learning is that people go through different phases and areas of interest. If a student stops learning, then we have a problem. But what is likely to happen is that the interest in rap music leads to an interest in other kinds of music, or in the business of music, or in the stories behind the lyrics, or in moving on to some other subject matter.

As John Dewey wrote, "There is, I think, no point in the philosophy of progressive education which is sounder than its emphasis upon the importance of the participation of the learner in the formation of the purposes which direct his activities in the learning process, just as there is no defect in traditional education greater than its failure to secure the active co-operation of the pupil in construction of the purposes involved in his studying."[7]

We also know that it is strengths of an individual that will increasingly become that person's advantage in the knowledge economy. The line of thinking is that we each should be learning what we are best at, not what we are worst at. We can debate that. But clearly what we know is that one of the primary goals of education in this century will be to help learners understand and develop their own unique talents, because in the knowledge economy it is uniqueness in talents, not commonality of skills, that is the key to successful and prosperous employment.

It is said that in the last century there were dozens of jobs for millions of people, and that in this century there will be millions of jobs for dozens of people. In the last century, we needed lots of people with the same skills. We needed lots of supervisors, lots of accountants, lots of farmers, and of course lots and lots of factory workers. In this century, we need just a few people in a whole lot more specialties, people with an increasingly diverse set of skills. In this century a company may only need one of these, and one of those occupational specialties. Thus we as educators need to help our learners identify and strengthen those individual strengths in knowledge and skill. And enhancing one's unique talents is now a higher priority than boosting one's weaknesses in a number of knowledge and skill areas.

The individually-tailored curriculum addresses the weaknesses in the existing limited curriculum. The individually-tailored curriculum:

1. Enhances each student's individual talents and abilities.
2. Encourages self-directed learning and necessarily involves the learner in setting her or his own learning goals.
3. Provides society with a greater number of skill and knowledge sets in its citizenry, so that the diverse and changing needs of business, work, defense and community can be met.
4. Maintains motivation and enthusiasm, keeping more students learning and moving forward intellectually.

5. Creates a structure in which future learning needs can be adopted and integrated into the curriculum.
6. Does not attempt to impose a given set of core subjects on every student, and does not attempt to make judgments about the value of subjects vis a vis each other. Instead, it allows the learner and teacher to create the best curriculum for the student.

Implementing an individually-tailored curriculum
There are two ways in which an individually-tailored curriculum will be implemented:
First, with the Web.
The web provides content, interaction and assessment tools so that students can learn anything. The web provides unlimited access to online teachers all over the world. So both online resources and online teachers can provide instruction in thousands of subject areas.
Second, with the Teacher.
By moving the role and function of the on-site teacher from teaching to helping students learn, teachers do not have to be subject-matter experts in order to help students learn.
The combination of online resources and teachers with face-to-face teachers serving as "guides on the side" can give each student an individually-tailored curriculum.

Learning contracts
The individually tailored curriculum gets created by having a learning contract, a model introduced by the educator Malcolm Knowles[8]. It is similar to an individual education plan (IEP), only it conducted for each and every student, it includes the student (and possibly his or her parents) in the decision-making process, and it does not imply any deficiency or abnormality.
The learning contract:
• Has the support and enthusiasm of the student.
• Can be for a short or long period of time.
• Can be changed at any time.
• Has teacher input, guidance and wisdom.
• Takes into account the student's "learning data" about his or her learning styles, progress, and current levels of knowledge.
• Allows for flexibility in speed and accomplishment, maturation changes.

Next stage learning

A learner moves on to the next level in a given subject area, or into another subject area, when she or he is ready for it. That is, the desire to learn and the motivation to study that particular subject need to be there for the learning to be maximized. We all have had experiences where we have been mandated to learn something, but most every educator and indeed learner confirms that when learning is voluntary, it is better.

Just-in-time learning has been prevalent in industry and business training for quite some time now. The idea is that the person learns something when she or he is ready to use it. That concept needs now to be applied to those in formal education as well. Of course, as long we think of a school or college as a factory, this will appear impossible. When we view all learning and education as personalized, then we reorient our thinking around how we can make that happen. Extending the notion of just-in-time learning for adults to learners in formal education is closely related to the "stage not age" concept that originated in the United Kingdom.

Stage not age

One of the aspects of education in the 21st century that we can already be fairly certain of is that learning will be based on "stage not age." We first heard of the concept when in the United Kingdom visiting with educators. "Stage Not Age" tests were cited by Ed Balls, Secretary of State for Schools, Children and Families, in his Children's Plan announced in Parliament in December 2007.[9]

In "stage not age" education going on the United Kingdom, educators are already realizing and beginning to implement the concept that students should study, be tested, and progress based on their "stage" of learning rather than on the student's age as it now exists in most schools.

The concept is already known among many K-12 teachers in the United States as well. In one K-12 seminar we did, "stage not age" was the top-rated change advocated by the teachers attending the seminar.

Age was the standard for the last century in the factory school. It made sense, industrially if not pedagogically, to treat all students the same, at the same time, in the same way, in order to prepare them for work in the factory.

But we know that we each learn differently, at different rates. And some of us learn one subject faster while needing more time on another subject.

The idea that every student should be on page 72 during week 5 of the course is simply not borne out by what we know about learning. We know some students are ahead while others need more time. When Julie was in school, she did very well in math in 1957. In that year the Russians launched Sputnik, the first spacecraft. That prompted a focus on math and science in the United States, which wanted to catch up in the space race. So Julie was promoted from seventh grade to ninth grade, skipping the eighth grade. In ninth grade she did very well, getting As in her subjects. But the "factory model" soon took over, and educators in her school realized that a 13-year-old was in the same classes as the 14-year-olds. That would not do.

Even though she got As on her gradecard, Julie was held back, in effect "flunked," and had to retake ninth grade all over again when her family moved to a new city, so that she would be with other students of the exact same age.

In summary, the limited curriculum and age-specific classes of the last century now appear to be obsolete.

Stage will replace age. In the 21st century school, students are almost certainly to be grouped, in-person and online, by their "stage" or level of learning, not be age. When a student achieves a given level of proficiency, that student moves on to the next level, or to another subject of study, regardless of his or her age. Stage learning will increase enthusiasm for learning; increase challenge in learning; take into account each learner's individual rate of learning and time needed for a particular subject; and help to maximize learning and the use of time by both student and teacher.

Limited subject curriculum will be replaced. Here we outlined three different models that have been proposed:

1. Flexible learning situations, in which a core curriculum is supplemented by 25% of school time devoted to other kinds of learning.
2. Process-oriented learning, in which students learn how to learn, focusing on the process of learning rather than subjects, with an emphasis on problem solving rather than mastering content.
3. Individually-tailored curriculum, in which 10,000 or so subjects

are available and each student has a learning contract outlining her or his learning goals and curriculum. Learning contracts will be universal. Regardless of the kind of curriculum or lack of it, all students will benefit from having an individual learning contract that is created in conjunction with the teacher, school, and parents for those learners under the legal age of majority. Learning contracts will take into account the student's current levels of knowledge and help personalize education by designing the best, most productive learning plan for the learner. They will be modified and changed whenever and as often as necessary.

Chapter 4.
From Pedagogy to Andragogy: The New Role for Teachers

Even with the incorporation of the Internet in instruction and education, the teacher becomes more important to a student's learning, not less important, in this century.[1] We are also likely to need more teachers in this century than we required in the last century.

The role and job description for most teachers will change dramatically. As John Dewey once said, "If we teach today's students as we taught yesterday's, we rob them of tomorrow." In this century, the first role of the teacher is to maintain and foster enthusiasm for learning. The second role of the teacher is to assist the student in her or his learning and knowledge.

The teacher should not be engaged in testing or evaluating a student's academic achievement. The teacher certainly should not be engaged in monitoring, supervising or instructing behavior. The teacher does not take attendance or do "classroom management." Some teachers may teach in the sense of being subject-matter experts; but what teachers really need to do is to help students learn.

As much as possible, the teacher moves from pedagogy to andragogy. Pedagogy is the art of teaching. Andragogy, a term coined by Malcolm Knowles, the father of adult education, is the art of learning. The teacher's role shifts from teaching to assisting each student to learn.[2] As Albert Einstein phrased it, "I never try to teach my students anything. I only try to create an environment in which they can learn."

So while teachers become even more important in this century, the role of the teacher and faculty member changes.

Student Teacher Ratios

Every study concludes that the teacher is the most important aspect of a person's learning. But there is no consensus on how many students that teacher should be instructing. Indeed, the assumed ideal limit of a 30:1 student to teacher ratio for education does not stand up to scrutiny, or classroom experience.[3]

For higher education, we know that more students in an online class can mean better, not lesser, learning. Certainly there is an excellent rationale for elementary school students to have fewer children per class. The rationale is that this allows the teacher to spend more time with each child, and that enhances their learning. But even in elementary and secondary education, having fewer students per class may not always maximize learning. It is a question for which we need more research.

As for the 30 student per class limit, the Baby Boom generation, born 1946 to 1964, did not experience any such ratio across the board in universities. There were simply too many students for the number of professors in the World War II and Silent Generation to teach. What universities did was to set up more chairs. There does not seem to be much documentation of the 30:1 ratio as ideal in the 1960s.

Classes of 200 to 600 students were not unusual. What was unusual about a class of 600 students was that the teacher was often a master guru, an extraordinary lecturer who brought insights and knowledge that average teachers did not possess.

There does not seem to be much evidence that the learning or workforce success of the Baby Boomer generation was penalized in any significant way from these large classes.

Then the Baby Boomer generation entered the workforce, and more specifically the teaching force, and the situation was largely reversed. We had a huge number of professors and instructors in colleges and universities, and a relatively smaller student body. This is how the 30:1 ratio economically had its rationale, as it would provide jobs for more teachers than if a larger class size was found to be acceptable.

When online classes began sprouting up in the late 1990s and early 2000s, educational experts tried, and succeeded for about five years, in enforcing the 30:1 ceiling in online courses. Without any evidence or rationale that online courses could not exceed 30 students, educators pronounced the 30 students-per-class ceiling as inviolable in the online classroom.

Beginning around 2005 we had enough evidence to challenge that ceiling from a student satisfaction standpoint. From the Certified Online Instructor (COI) program[4], we required instructors to get student ratings of their online courses as part of the certification process. By studying the results, it was clear that there was no quality difference from the student's standpoint between online classes with more than 30 students and those with 30 or fewer students.

About the same time, more and more institutions began ignoring the 30-student ceiling and allowed additional students in the online classes, so that by 2009 some instructors were reporting 100 students in their online classes.

The third thing that happened, or did not happen, is that there were no studies showing that student achievement declined when online classes had more than 30 students in them.

We are clear that more of the teacher's time has to be spent in interaction with students. Only 55% of the average instructor's time is devoted to actually teaching, according to the U.S. Department of Education. That percentage has to rise to 75% or more.

But at the same time, one of the top priorities and biggest challenges educationally in the 21st century in post-industrial countries is to have fully half of their youth receive four-year college degrees and thus be eligible to become knowledge workers.

Through increasing teacher contact time, specialization of teacher roles, and online delivery of content, both aims can be achieved. Students can get more instructor contact, and society can produce more college graduates.

That cannot be done, however, with the existing classroom model.

The 30-students-per-class rationale for online classes has disintegrated with experience and evaluations of thousands of online courses with more than 30 students. So too may the 30-students-per-class rationale for in-person class meetings also be revisited. Certainly some courses benefit from more full professor face time or individual attention than others.

Increasing Time with Students

Regardless of the size of the class, a primary goal of education should be to increase teacher and faculty time with students, not diminish it. Here are some 21st century ways to increase faculty time with students:

- **Online discussion.** With online discussion, instructors can engage with more students in a more time-efficient manner than in-person conversation.
- **Reduction of meeting time.** Faculty today spends way too much time in meetings and non-essential administrative duties. By reducing meeting time, faculty can allocate more time to be spent with students.
- **Time in transport reduced.** Faculty time can also be maximized by not spending as much time driving cars, leaving more time to spend with students.
- **Specialization.** Instructors trained in a teaching specialty like andragogy, needs assessment or evaluation/grading can handle more students per instructor than 'generalist' faculty who have to perform a variety of tasks with different skill sets, in which they are not as proficient or effective.[5]
- **Network of people.** Students have always had these resources, but they have not been intentionally identified, nurtured or encouraged[6]. Peers, parents and elders, and professionals can and should be incorporated into a network of human resources for students. This is in addition to a teaching team (SME, andragogy, discussion facilitator + counselor, grader/tester).
- **Learning data.** In this century, the student, his or her parents if the student is under the age of majority, and teachers will have - must have - enormous amounts of learning data specific to the individual learner. This learning data will enhance the student's learning, but also help teachers make more efficient use of their time in helping to enhance that learning.[7]

Generalist vs Specialist Teachers

The generalist teacher is probably no longer as efficient or as effective as the specialist teacher. With teaching, however, "generalist" and "specialist" do not refer just to content or subject matter; they also include the pedagogical role the person plays in student learning.

In general, generalists in the workplace are being replaced by specialists. For example, when our organization had a national headquarters office, we had, like other businesses and organizations, mainly full-time people. Full-time people were assigned an average of six different responsibilities. Each required a different skill set. Each required only about 10% to 20% of the person's time. And no person, in our experience, had equal strengths in all six areas. A person was generally hired for one or two outstanding skill sets, and then given four or so other responsibilities because someone had to do them, or they came with the job.

One of your authors' full-time staff members had the job of negotiating the contract with the hotel for our annual conference. He performed the function well, we thought. And then that person left our organization, we became virtual, and we looked at specialists in a number of areas. We contracted with Bill Strehl, a man half-way across the country, just to negotiate our hotel contracts and work with the hotels during our conferences. At our first conference, he asked us for $1,000 in small bills. We said we didn't do that sort of thing. He said, "Give me the money," which we did. After the conference was over, the hotel bill was $4,000 less than it had been in previous years. Mr. Strehl did not just save our organization money; he also increased the quality of our conferences. We stayed with the hotel specialist thereafter.

The same is true for faculty. Faculty members don't just "teach." They engage in a number of different activities, each with a different skill set. They are subject-matter specialists. They are lecturers and presenters of material and content. They are discussion leaders. They should be helping students to learn. They occasionally are asked to engage in academic counseling by some students. And of course, they evaluate student learning and give out grades.

In this century another teaching function will be added, that of needs assessment and pre-course testing.

Like the full-time people in our office, like many full-time people and generalists in all kinds of occupations and settings, the faculty member of the last century was a generalist. Like other people, no one faculty member can or should be expected to excel in all seven areas of teaching skills.

Like what is happening in other occupations and professions, it is likely and beneficial if faculty members specialize in one, perhaps two of the following:

1. Subject-matter specialist
2. Lecturer and presenter of content
3. Discussion facilitator
4. Andragogy, helping students to learn
5. Needs assessment and pre-course testing

41

6. Knowledge evaluation and grading
7. Academic advising
The big three areas:

Assessment, which must be contracted out to an independent source to provide objective measurement of learning and knowledge.

Andragogy and discussion, an orientation almost totally devoted to the needs and learning styles of the student rather than to any mastery of the content (a totally optional skill set for this aspect of teaching).

Content, the traditional role most faculty members see as their primary job responsibility (which is why geography faculty members go to the national geography conference, and not to the national andragogy conference).

The real work, the real challenge, the real make-or-break aspect of teaching, is in the andragogy - the area of helping students to learn.

Chapter 5.
Learning and Teaching: The 21 Pedagogical Concepts

Here is our preliminary list of the 21 most important pedagogical concepts for the 21st century. It is "preliminary" because at the time of this writing, neither we nor other educators know, or should pretend to know, everything about education in the 21st century.

Some of the pedagogical concepts are new, some of them are old, none of them were highly regarded in the factory-model school of the last century. The list, in no particular order and no priority assigned, is sure to change somewhat, with a couple of the concepts fading and replaced by a couple of pedagogical concepts not yet recognized or even invented yet. Yet the majority of these concepts will drive an entirely different kind of learning and teaching. These concepts will also, in the main, be the basis on which educators reconfigure schools and colleges in the 21st century.

1. Collaborative learning

What we know is that in this century, a group working together at the same time, either synchronously or asynchronously, can produce more of higher quality, than a single individual can produce.

In the last century, individuals worked essentially alone. They all worked with others of course, in the factory, store, office or other place of work. But "working" was something you did by yourself, not with the help of others.

As an office manager, Bill remembers that if two people were talking together in the office, it was presumed they were socializing and not working. So he would give them about 3-5 minutes, and then go over to them and suggest they "go back to work."

There was "teamwork." But teamwork meant each person doing his or her own job, and together that produced a result. Teams were almost never evaluated nor rewarded as a team. It was individuals who were evaluated and rewarded.

In the last century, individuals studied essentially alone. Study was preparation for work, but study was also regarded as work. Study was never play. When we were growing up, we had to study alone. We even had to study with our feet on the floor. You couldn't study lying down in bed, for example. That was not taking your studies, your work, seriously enough. And of course individuals were evaluated and graded based upon their individual performance. Rarely would there be a group grade.

Collaboration means everyone doing the same job at essentially the same time. In this century the world is so complicated, the competition so intense, specialization and niche fields so numerous, the problems so huge, that a group can be more productive in many instances than an individual. That is, a group can be more creative, more inventive, more productive and more profitable than a single individual working alone.

Here's a true story. A company decided to create a puzzle on its web site and offer $25,000 to the first person who solved the puzzle. They figured the winner would take about 30 days to figure out the puzzle. During those 30 days, the company would make a lot of money with banner ads, selling t-shirts and whatever to those people playing the puzzle game. What they did not count on was something called "smart mobs." A smart mob is a group of people who get together to work on problems. A smart mob discovered the puzzle game, solved it in just three days, and won the $25,000 prize, shutting down the web site which lost money because they could not sell enough stuff to cover the prize money in just three days.

People coming into the workforce in the 21st century will want and need to be able to work collaboratively with others. We do not know what percentage of their work time will be spent working collaboratively with others, but we do know that at least some of their time will be spent working collaboratively. So collaborative learning helps prepare people for working collaboratively.

The other reason why collaborative learning is an important new pedagogy for the 21st century is that collaborative learning can be more effective than studying on one's own in some or many instances.

For those teaching and learning in the last century, collaborative learning may appear to be cheating. As Milwaukee futurist Richard Thieme said, "They call it collaborative learning. When I was growing up, they called it cheating."[1]

Collaborative work and learning can take place face-to-face. But the distinguishing new feature of collaborative work and learning for this century is that of virtual teams, people who work and/or learn collaboratively at distances from each other.

The beauty of the virtual team is that team members can be recruited from any geographic location in the world, and therefore can be chosen for the particular expertise, knowledge or skill that each one brings to the virtual team. Thus the virtual team can be more powerful, productive, inventive, creative and powerful, than a team that depends only on individuals within a given geographic location.

Open neighbor tests

Julie discovered one of the first Gen Y teachers. She was Laura Taylor, then age 24, who taught mathematics at North Carolina State University in Raleigh.

Ms. Taylor gave "open neighbor" tests. You may have heard of "open book" tests, where one can look at the book during the test. You could not look at the book during one of Ms. Taylor's tests. But you could talk to your neighbor.[2]

For many older faculty members, this is called cheating. But Ms. Taylor was a statistician and math teacher. She discovered that when students took open neighbor tests, they did better on the final exams, which were neither open neighbor nor open book, than students who did not take open neighbor tests.

Ms. Taylor believed her job was to teach math. So she employed those techniques, including collaborative test-taking, which would improve the learning and knowledge skills of her students.

Open neighbor tests are just one way that collaborative learning can be utilized in the classroom.

2. Learning goes online

In the 21st century, every course of study will have an online component. Half of all learning will be online.[3]

There will be many, many courses with a face-to-face component, especially at the elementary and secondary levels, and for undergraduates under age 25; but every course, whether it meets in-person or not, will have an online component. And of course many, many courses will be completely online, with no in-person meetings.

At the time of this writing, the question for most courses is whether to put some aspect or the entire course online. There are currently face-to-face or traditional classroom courses, online courses, and hybrid courses. Alternative names for hybrid courses include web-enhanced and mixed. Teachers consider whether to put their course online, or what portion of the course to put online.

We are currently in a transition period. Eventually we will wind up where every course of study is online, and teachers will consider whether to have a face-to-face component to supplement and enhance the online aspect of the course.

Almost all knowledge workers do their work online. Learning in school and college has to be online, because future workers have to learn online skills in order to effectively communicate, work, and be productive in the work world.

For the past ten to fifteen years, the quality of online learning has been documented as having "no significant difference" from traditional classroom courses. More recently, however, the first studies have been done indicating that courses including online learning may be superior to in-person only courses.[4]

3. Resources outside of the school

Throughout most of modern history, schools and libraries have been the primary if not major repository for knowledge resources. For the first time in centuries, more learning and knowledge resources exist outside of the school or college than inside.[5]

Generation Y is the first generation to experience this dramatic change. By going online, learners and teachers can gain access to the greater portion of those resources. To attempt to gain subject-matter mastery and knowledge skills without using the Internet is now quite unthinkable.

Teachers, schools and colleges have to not just accept, but embrace the notion and reality that most knowledge resources exist outside of school and college. In the United Kingdom, for example, one major concern of the education department there is access to the Internet for children when they are outside of school. This is positive thinking that encompasses the entire learning environment, and helps to position schools and colleges in their new role in that environment.

4. Learners create content

In the 21st century, students do not just learn content, they also create content.

The web has enabled learners to create content. And Gen Y - interactive, involved, a "do it" generation - can and wants to create content. At the time of this writing, the concept is called Web 2.0. Using software programs on the web, people not only access content and information, but they contribute content and information.

One of the first applications of Web 2.0 was Wikipedia, the online encyclopedia which, within five years of its creation, became equal to or surpassed the centuries-old Encyclopedia Britannica, the most respected name in encyclopedias.

Then came Flickr, where people can post pictures on the web.

Then came YouTube, where people can post videos on the web.

Then came various mapping software options, where people create maps not previously made before.

Then came various software programs called "mash ups," where two or more interactive software programs were utilized to create multi-dimensional outcomes, such as video maps.

And so on.

The end result of all this people participation is content that has never been created or collected or distributed before.

Now some of you are reading this and thinking this is relevant and applies to your area of knowledge and teaching. And some of you are reading this and think that this has no relevance or applicability to your subject matter or teaching. You might be teaching basic math, and it is unlikely your students will revise 2+2. You might be teaching the history of World War II, and it is unlikely your learners will change the outcome of the Battle of the Bulge.

But creating content does not simply mean creating original new content, although it certainly includes the creation of new ideas and original content.

Involving your learners in creating content can have these positive variations.

Asking original or new questions

Participants move learning and teaching to a new level not just by offering "answers," but also by providing questions. The way a question is phrased, the implication in the question, the new direction a question takes the group, and the questions themselves all are integral to creating content. Questions are often more important than the answers, and lead the learning exploration in many ways.

Elucidating needs and wants
Learner needs and wants continue to change, evolve and adapt to new situations. Students will help teachers modify content by explaining their needs and wants. Applications, relevance, and validity of content to new situations and environments create a seemingly never-ending role for learners to keep content fresh and relevant.
Explaining content in new and original ways
Learners are some of the best teachers. When a learner explains content to someone else in the class, that person may do it in new and original ways. As language changes and new generations have different backgrounds and experiences, there is an ongoing need to find new ways to explain content to learners.

Customizing content for specific audiences
There is much to know; but there are also many audiences and learners from a growing number of different backgrounds, learning styles, abilities and disabilities. All these different kinds of learners are in distinct "niches" or "markets." We do not currently have a term specific to education for various learner audiences, so we will borrow the terms from business.
To illustrate, is there an approach to teaching algebra for Hmong people in the United States with kinetic learning styles?
Learners will help teachers create new ways to help themselves and other learners gain knowledge by helping teachers customize content for specific audiences.

5. Learning from your students
Good teachers always learn something from their participants. In the 21st century, learning from your participants may be a prerequisite to good teaching.
We know that anyone born before 1980 can benefit from learning about technology and the Internet from younger people. For the Gen X and Baby Boom generations, the last pre-21st century generations, people born in or after 1980 inherently know more about technology than their elders. Not only that, but by the time an older person learns

a particular technology, the younger person has already learned two to three times as much. Donald Tapscott, in his book *Growing Up Digital*, calls this "lapping."[6] Most older people will never be able to catch up technology-wise to younger people. If you were born before 1980 and enjoy learning about technology, good for you. Keep it up. We do not know if this will always be the case for future generations. We do not know if Generation Y teachers will benefit from learning from the next generation about technology, or whether Gen Y and other 21st century generations will be equal in technology adoption.

We do know that Gen Y teachers and all teachers in the 21st century will benefit from learning from the kids[7]. Respect for the elders in the community has been a traditional value for centuries. But there is also an Ojibway saying: "Respect the young people because they are closer in time to the Creator."

Learning to ask questions

Learn to ask questions. Asking questions is a skill not too many people have acquired. Reporters are trained to ask questions. In journalism school they learn to ask about Who, What, Where, When, Why and How.

Continually ask questions of your learners. Ask them why they said that, why they did or did not do something. If you follow up your initial question with another question, that will demonstrate you are paying attention. It also will get you more in-depth information and perspective. Ask your questions in the neutral voice of a reporter doing a story. If the tone of your voice is judgmental or gives away your feelings, the individual will become defensive. Then reward or thank the person for answering your question. Always let the person know you appreciate that he/she responded, regardless of their response.

6. Peak learning time

Learning and teaching becomes a 24-hour activity every day in this century. Schools will need to be open 18 hours a day for both pedagogical and financial reasons. But students will be learning anytime day or night, and teachers will be "on the job" and "on the clock" 24 hours a day.

Schools in the last century started and ended at about the same time as the first shift of the factory. The rural one-room schoolhouse of the agrarian age also was primarily in session during daylight hours, but for a slightly different reason. It had to respond to the seasons and the needs of farming. This is an often- cited reason why schools are not in session during the summer, the time when the crops must be planted and harvested. And Julie notes that while she was growing up, her school would often be dismissed at other times of the year for a day or two so that the tobacco crops could be harvested.

In the early part of the 20th century, some model schools in Gary, Indiana, also experimented with having a second shift in the afternoon and evening.

In this century, we know that people do not all have the same peak work or learning time. Peak work or learning time is the hour or hours of the day or night when a person is most productive, when his or her mind functions best, when both the quantity and quality of work or learning is better than if performed at another time of day or night.

Here's an illustration. When our organization became virtual, we dismantled our national headquarters office and allowed staff to move and live wherever they wanted. One of our employees, Danita, moved from Kansas to Michigan and then to Nebraska and then to Colorado and then to Minnesota and then back to Colorado. Five years later, Bill told Danita that he had thought she would only stay with our organization five or six months after we went virtual, because with another employer she could work face-to-face with other people. To his amazement, Danita said she stayed with our organization because we were one of the few places where she could work at 3 a.m. Bill had no idea she worked at 3 a.m. because she always responded to emails and other communication promptly. As an employer, we then realized that we wanted her to work at 3 a.m. because she was obviously most productive at that hour. And if she was most productive, then our organization was more profitable if our people worked when they wanted.

A study of when people said they were most productive revealed the fascinating details. Some 50% of people say they are most productive in the morning. Another 25% of people say they are most productive in the afternoon. But fully 20% of people say they are most productive in the evening, after the typical work day ends. And then 6% of people (numbers are rounded) say they are most productive in the night-time hours.

What that means is that employers shut the gates, lock the doors, and send their workers home at the moment that 26% of the workforce is just starting to be most productive. That is simply too unproductive, too unprofitable, and too uncompetitive for organizations in an increasingly competitive business environment.

We know that teenagers are active in the evening and at night, and that it is actually healthier for them to sleep later in the morning. Based on that research, the Minneapolis public school system was one of the first to move the starting time for high school back to 9 a.m., and then documented that student achievement went up after the school start time was changed.

Peak work and learning time may change according to one's age, but it does not change uniformly for everyone.

Not every teacher will need to work at midnight, but some teachers also will be most productive at night and be hired to teach at night.

With the Internet, online teachers and advisors can be located in other time zones, thus responding to students during evening and night-time hours.

The end result will be that peak learning time will enhance each and every student's academic performance.

7. Peak learning place

When our educational association had a central national headquarters office in Kansas in the 1990s, we had some natural staff turnover. So we started to recruit new people to fill our vacancies. We called Paul in Portland, Oregon, and asked Paul to work for LERN. He said great. We said move to our national headquarters office. He said no. We asked about Denver, Santa Fe, Seattle, San Francisco. He said no.

We called Greg in Providence, Rhode Island, and invited Greg to join the national headquarters staff. Greg said yes. We said move to our national headquarters office. He said no. We asked about Chicago, Philadelphia, New York, and Cleveland. He said no.

We became a virtual organization and got Paul and Greg on staff, but they stayed in Portland and Providence respectively.

It was only a few years later that we fully understood that in the knowledge economy of the 21st century, you do not want your best people to move. You want your best people to be located in the place where they are most creative, innovative and productive. We discovered that when we ourselves moved to a place where we could be more productive.

Likewise, you want your students to be learning in the place, or places, where they are most creative, innovative and productive. This place is not always the school building. This place may change over time, over the time of day, and there may be several places where a given individual has the environment that maximizes his or her learning and knowledge acquisition.

So while we will still have classes, still have meetings of the teacher and students, those meetings will not constitute the entirety of the "school day." Individuals will be scheduled during the school day to be in other places at various times of the day and week.

In the factory model school of the last century, learning took place in only one place, a desk with other students in a classroom. In this century, teachers, schools and colleges need to help learners choose those places in which they can learn best.

8. Self-discipline

When our son Willie was young, the famous rap artist Tupac Shakur was murdered. But Willie found a web site that proved that Tupac was still alive. If you added his social security number and his street address, and divided by his astrological sign, that was proof that Tupac was still alive. As parents we were dumbfounded. We had no idea what to say. So we said nothing. Every day for two weeks, Willie came to us with more "evidence" that Tupac was still alive. Finally he stopped telling us, and apparently stopped visiting the web site. In retrospect, we think what was going on was Willie as a young person trying to figure out what was right and what was wrong on the Internet. He was developing judgment skills and self-discipline in terms of learning and working online.

In the 21st century, there are no gate-keepers to knowledge. Growing up in the last century, we had gate keepers. The doctor told us what illness we had. The minister told us what to believe. And every evening, the television newsman Walter Cronkite ended his broadcast by saying, "And that's the way it is." And that was the way it was.

Today those gate-keepers are gone. Today when Julie becomes ill, she goes online and then discusses with her doctor what the cause and cure might be. Today we get news sources from all over, and have to decide for ourselves what is real and not real.

And so every person in the 21st century has to form the skills of both judgment and self-discipline in both learning and in work.

While adults may say they are self-disciplined, in reality people raised in the last century were not taught or generally experienced self-discipline. In our formal societal institutions, discipline almost always came from someone else. In the last century, teachers supervised our education. In the workplace, everyone except the boss had a supervisor. One of the critical skills those working in the 21st century will need to have is self-discipline. In knowledge work, there are few supervisors. In the workplace, "supervisor" is a job title that is a relic of the last century. Knowledge workers have to be self-disciplined enough to meet deadlines, meet quality standards, and motivate themselves.

Can teachers who have always had supervisors teach self-discipline and judgment skills to students who will never have supervisors?

Individuals in this century will learn self-discipline and judgment skills because they are absolutely essential in the workplace. As teachers we can help, but we cannot supervise.

One of the ways in which we help children and youth with self-discipline is to give them control over increasing amounts of their own time. Another way will be to give them control over their own decision-making.

No four-year-old will be given complete control over his or her own time, nor will a 40-year-old learner. But for children and youth, teachers at various stages (stages, not ages) will start with small amounts of time during the day and allow the child to use it as she or he will. As the child grows older and matures, an increasing amount of time will be turned over the student. In this way children learn from a young age about disciplining their time.

Likewise, teachers will give learners control over their own decision making with regards to their learning. Again, this will start small and grow large.

When we were young, our uncle Bob was a doctor with a black bag. He could diagnose and cure just about any illness we had. Years later, as adults, we went to the doctor. The doctor would bring out not a black bag but a huge black book, and say, "Let's find out what you have." And today our doctor walks in and she says, "What do you think you have?" In much the same way, teaching has to progress through these same stages to the point where we as teachers work with our learners in deciding about what and how to learn.

Our interactions with doctors are a cooperative exploration, communication, and decision-making process. Learners need to know more about their own learning style than anyone else. Learners and teachers need to cooperate in exploration, communication and decision-making about education.

9. Every Student is Treated Differently

In the last century, educators believed that equal treatment meant treating each student the same. In this century, teachers and institutions will treat each student differently, not the same. If each of us is different (we are), then as learners we should each be treated differently in order to maximize our learning and our skills. Currently, educators proudly proclaim "We treat each student the same." Treating students the same is supposed to ensure that students are treated equally. And that made sense when students were being prepared for the factory, where all the workers were, and had to be, treated the same.

In this century treating students the same means treating them unequally, not equally. Now treating students equally means treating them differently, not the same. Treating a student with autism the same as a student without autism makes no sense. Likewise, it makes no pedagogical sense to treat a student who excels in math and is three stages ahead of other students of the same age the same as treating a student who needs assistance and is three stages behind other students of the same age.

One way we will treat students differently is to have a learning contract, such as the one advocated for adults by Malcolm Knowles[8]. In schools today educators have an IEP, or individualized education plan, mandated by the Individuals with Disabilities Act. With no one being normal, and every person having one or more weaknesses, think of a learning contract as an IEP for every student.

10. Learning Environments

The entirety of the physical space creates a learning environment. Some kinds of learning environments impact some learners positively, others negatively. The Department of Education in the United States reported that the physical environment can impact 25% of the learning that takes place.

You can use learning environments to enhance the learning of individuals in a group. You can also help individual learners design or enhance their own personal learning environment at home or in another location to maximize their learning.

Willie took an SAT test and got a pretty good score. But when Willie took an advanced writing SAT test, he requested and received extended time. And then when we arrived at the school for testing, a smart alert teacher supervising the exam asked Willie if he wanted to be in a room with windows or no windows. Willie's test score improved significantly after being given extended time and the learning environment of his choice.

This is what teachers and schools in the 21st century are supposed to do: maximize the academic performance of each student. In the last century, it was important to have everyone perform in the same environment, because there was only one environment in the factory and office.

In the last century the "same" environment was judged to be "equal and fair." We know that is not, and was not, so. Today we know that "same" does not mean equal or fair, because the same environment does not impact each person in the same way. Willie did not receive an "unfair" advantage. He received an environment which maximized his productivity. Every learner needs to receive the environment, learning mediums, and teaching that enhance her or his learning.

K-12 teachers, especially elementary school teachers, are excellent at designing physical environments for their students. For example, "Unlike children almost everywhere, those in Ms. Brown's class do not have to sit and be still. Quite the contrary, they may stand and fidget all class long if they want. And they do."[9] The story relates how Abby Brown created stand-up desks so her students could stand or sit when they wish. The stand-up desks come with swinging footrests, and with adjustable stools allowing children to switch between sitting and standing as their moods dictate.

Learning mediums are physical objects in the environment that aid in learning. Examples of learning mediums are flowers, special kinds of music, posters, scents and aromas, ribbons, mints, food and drink, and so on. These subtle but helpful aids in learning often work very quietly. Many learners are not even aware of their presence, and others are not conscious of their intent as learning aids.

- The sight of flowers stimulates people to be more receptive and positive when entering the room.
- Music has aided learning. The Lind Institute in San Francisco produces classical music set to the beats of the heart, and this special kind of music enhances learning.
- Posters on the wall send positive and reinforcing messages to learners.
- Ribbons for meeting attendees provide a little extra self esteem

with the recognition.
- Food and drink have various stimulating properties for certain kinds of audiences at certain times of the day.

In the last century, learning mediums, when they were used at all, were intended to affect everyone in the class or group.

In this century, you should also use learning mediums on an individual basis.

Because not all of your learners have the same learning style, respond in the same way to the same colors, environments, physical objects or other learning mediums, you will want to customize and tailor the learning mediums to each individual.

How many learning mediums to use, when, and how often, will all need to be discovered. What we know now is that learning mediums do enhance learning.

We know colors affect individuals, and groups of people in various occupations and entire cultures, in different ways. A particular color is perceived in a certain way, positively, negatively, creating calm, excitement, resentment, uncertainty, anxiety and other emotions.

We also know that certain kinds of animals and pets can positively influence learning. Those people with Asperger's and other forms of autism will be significantly assisted when a dog or other pet is present and can be petted. The pet has a calming affect that allows the person to focus and concentrate on learning.

When Willie enrolled in a new high school, we took him around to meet his teachers. When it came to his new study hall teacher, Willie asked whether he could listen to music with his headphones while studying. The teacher said no. Being a good teacher, she reversed her decision the next day and allowed music if it did not disturb anyone else.

11. Gaming

Three events occurred around 2005 that made it clear that working, and thus learning, in virtual worlds would be central if not essential in the 21st century.

The first event was the first person to purchase a virtual island in a virtual world, with real money. Some $22,000 was paid by the Australian young man for the island. What he did with it is now obvious, but at the time it was quite astonishing. He divided up his virtual island, sold real estate property on the beach, built virtual houses for people on their virtual beachfront property, and within a year had recouped his initial investment. One unexpected source of income was renting land for virtual hunting of virtual wildlife. With this move, he was the first person to demonstrate that virtual worlds are both "real" and economic or financial places. So the virtual world is now an economic reality.

The second event was a study conducted by Dr. James Clarence Rosser, a New York surgeon. The headline in the *New York Times* was a classic pedagogical revelation, "We have to operate, but let's play first."

We have been teaching faculty to teach online since 2000. While there is a little resistance to the idea today, in 2000 there was much reluctance, doubtfulness, and challenging of online teaching. A professor would log on and say that you can't teach French online. And then another faculty member would log on and say that actually she teaches French online, and you can do these wonderful audio clips. Then an instructor would log on and say that you can't teach music online. And then another professor would log on and say that actually he teaches music online, and you can separate the treble from the bass online. And then a bunch of faculty would pound out the definitive declaration, "well, I wouldn't want to be operated on by a doctor who learned surgery online." That, supposedly was unassailable and undeniable. Well apparently.....

So Dr. Rosser plays video games in between doing surgery. Apparently patients do not rupture their organs in a timely sequential manner, so surgeries cannot always be scheduled in a row all day; thus there is down-time for a surgeon. Dr. Rosser plays video games because it increases his manual dexterity, although we also believe there is something positive in addition going on that enhances his surgical skills. Then Dr. Rosser decided to do a survey of other doctors who play video games. He discovered that doctors who play video games make 37% fewer mistakes than doctors who do not play video games. Lesson number two is that playing games in the virtual world increases productivity, accuracy, and skill sets.[10]

The third event was the making of a new airplane by a French airplane company. Apparently up until then all new models of airplanes needed to have a prototype, a physical replica of the new plane. The prototype was built before the first real airplane was constructed, in order to work out the bugs and problems in advance.[11]

The French airplane company built its new airplane without a prototype. Instead, it built the new plane totally in cyberspace. Virtual people worked in the plane to see how that went. Interior decorating designs were created and evaluated. And the plane even "flew" in cyberspace, testing such things as wind speed, banking and every other aspect of flying a plane. Then, they built the first airplane and flew it. The test pilot reported after the first flight that it flew just like in cyberspace. The advantage to the French company in building the plane in cyberspace and without a prototype is that the company was able to cut its development costs in half, a savings of hundreds of millions of dollars. Lesson number three is that gaming in the virtual world is profitable.

The final lesson is for individuals and organizations that do not do gaming in the virtual world. You cannot compete with individuals and organizations that do gaming in the virtual world, because they will have lower costs and greater productivity or accuracy.

Throughout history, play has always been a rehearsal for life as an adult. Once again, video game, online gaming, and virtual world activities demonstrate this axiom.

So knowledge workers in the 21st century will rehearse with gaming in virtual worlds before they perform the actual activity in the physical world. Lawyers will rehearse the court trial in cyberspace, making all kinds of stupid assertions and getting overruled, because when they walk into the real courtroom they will be better able to win the case. Doctors, accountants, artists, and every other profession will engage in the same kind of preparation and rehearsal.

Even teachers will teach in cyberspace, rehearsing techniques to figure out which ones will work with which learners, what will enhance the learning, and what actions will be a big mistake with other kinds of individuals.

We will need to distinguish between cyberspace that is meant for practice and rehearsal, and virtual worlds where real people are interacting with each other. We do not practice on avatars, because avatars are real people, with emotions, feelings, and mental states that can be negatively affected.

We will practice in cyberspace with 'bots, mechanical preprogrammed virtual characters that do not represent real people.

For example, some teachers will go into cyber classrooms with bots as students, unreal characters who perform according to a set of data. Teachers will practice saying something to a student by trying it out on a bot to determine whether, based on the experience of hundreds of thousands of teachers with millions of students, a certain phrase or action works with a particular kind of student. Instead of experimenting on a real person, trying something out with a bot will help teachers prepare for live interaction with real students, especially for those new situations that even the most experienced teacher may encounter. Cyberspace won't make the real world perfect, but it will greatly reduce risk and boost the chances for success.

12. Another identity

We were sitting in a session on virtual world gaming at a university conference with the faculty presenter, a middle-aged man with wife and children. When he showed us his avatar, an 18-year-old girl, the room was silent. We all sat there a little stunned, not knowing how to react, internally trying to assess whether this was somehow unethical or immoral or what. He then described how other avatars treated him differently as a female than as a male avatar, and how that different identity allowed him to see things differently.

"When you lived in only one community, like a village 250 years ago, you had one identity," Swiss author and educator Etienne Wenger notes. But with each individual involved and engaged in so many different communities, both physical and online, today, there is a necessity to manage your identity that did not exist before.

To deal with all three issues, Wenger suggested that knowledge has to shift "from curriculum to the construction of a person" and that educators have to understand that knowledge evolves from practice and experience, not from the classroom.[12]

13. Learning at home

We have to assume that learners will spend significant amounts of time during the formal school day learning at home. No student will spend six hours a day, five days a week, in a school or college. Learning takes some individual time, some time working collaboratively online, some study time, some online time absorbing content and listening to lectures, some time online discussing with other peers and with one or more teachers, some time online each and every week in assessment, whether it be ungraded self-quizzes or unit tests. Learning at home is also preparation for work, where most all college graduates will work at home, or anywhere, or everywhere.

The notion that a teacher must be present at all times, that the only place where learning occurs is in a classroom, that learners have to be monitored and supervised while being online, that no student should or can be disciplined enough to work on her or his own, simply does not lead to the outcomes demanded by the post-industrial workplace, nor does it utilize the resources now available for learning. The home-schooling movement has demonstrated that people can learn at home, can learn online, and that classroom management is not a significant issue for homeschooled children.

The factory model of school also assumes that parents are at the factory during the day. This is becoming an increasingly invalid assumption. In this century, elementary and secondary school students will spend anywhere from one to three days a week studying at home, or at a friend's house, or a relative's house, or at the coffeehouse, or at the public library, or in a study room such as the library at the school.

When he was a child in the early part of the twentieth century, Landon Divers had free rail passes because his father worked for the railroad. If he made sure his homework was done, or would be done on time, the school would allow him time off during the school day to take the train 60 miles to Milwaukee, where he would see a play or a movie, and return home by nightfall.[13] That kind of student mobility and use of time will return again in our education.

14. Continuous engagement

Online instructors are pioneering a number of the new concepts in teaching. One of those instructors is Dr. Mary Dereshiwsky of Northern Arizona University, who created the concept of "continuous engagement."

For an online teacher, continuous engagement means always being perceived as available to the students, being responsive to their needs and questions, always being positive and enthusiastic, and always being helpful.

The concept of continuous engagement can be applied to the in-person or face-to-face teacher as well. While a teacher obviously cannot be available to one's students 24 hours a day, it is the perception of being available which makes the difference. It moves the teacher another step closer to being there with one's students whenever they need the instructor. It moves faculty one step farther away from being the sage on the stage, and another step closer to being the guide on the side.

It also reinforces the need for teachers to have more engagement time with students, with a greater proportion of their work time being spent with students.

15. Peer engagement

The concept of peer engagement is that learners help each other to learn. This concept goes back more than a hundred years in formal schools. In the rural one-room schoolhouse, the teacher would ask older students to help younger ones with their studies. In some ways the class of the 21st century greatly resembles the class of the one-room schoolhouse. In the one-room school house there were children from all grades, one through eight, in the same room. Thus there were students with various degrees of mastery, maturity, and accomplishment. The teacher routinely called upon the older students to help the younger ones. As today, girls were generally one to two years more along in maturity, and they were more often used in helping the others.

In today's class, we also have people of differing abilities, levels of achievement and accomplishment. The range may not be as great as the one-through-eighth grade situation, yet in every class some students are ahead of others, some are a little behind, one or two may be way ahead, and one or two way behind.

In the factory school of the last century, having individuals in different places was a problem. In this century, it is both an omnipresent reality and an opportunity.

The first thing we need to acknowledge is that our learners are in different places at any given time, learn at different rates of speed, and have differing abilities.

The bell curve of human activity would indicate that in most classes most students will not vary significantly in ability, speed, and knowledge progression. There will be students at either end of the bell curve, some with much higher ability, faster learning speed, and greater knowledge achievement. And there will be some at the other end, with less ability, slower learning speed, and less knowledge achievement.

This situation is no longer a teaching challenge. We clearly cannot continue to categorize learners as "normal" and fitting the norm, and those at either end who do not fit. That view of our students worked when preparing or returning to the factory, but no longer.

As teachers, we now need to see this variation as a positive and a learning resource.

16. Learning data

There are certain frontiers of learning and education that are exciting new areas of exploration in this century. The neurology of learning is one. Online learning is another. Another one is certainly going to be what we call "learning data." "Traces are now computable," says Swiss author and educator Etienne Wenger.[14]

We suggest that learning data will be an ever greater accumulation of data about an individual's learning. Think of it like that huge bulky manila folder with medical data about you that the doctor opens up when you have a doctor's appointment. That huge bulky folder with medical data about you is, at the time of this writing, in the process of going online.

Online medical data will have many beneficial effects, but here are two.

One, you will be healthier. When you are travelling or in another location, you will want another doctor or hospital to have access to your medical records, so they can better treat you for some illness or injury. That's the first thing most people think about when it comes to the benefits of online medical records.

But there's more. One, you will have access to those records, and you can assist in your own diagnosis, behavior modification, and self-treatment by having access to all of your medical data. Having had many experiences with doctors, illness and treatment over a lifetime, Julie says she - not any single doctor - knows the most about her own health because she has spent the most time studying it. She has proven that to every physician who has become her primary doctor. Now Julie and her doctor work together on her health.

So too will the learner be seen as the single person with the most understanding of that person's learning. By accessing your own learning data, you will better be able to enhance your learning, professional and personal development. And every student will be able to do the same.

Two, others will be healthier. The second major benefit of putting medical records online is that others will become healthier. When the medical records of millions of people are put online, cumulative data emerges that could not be foreseen by simply looking at millions of individual medical records. So your medical data goes into a huge pot of data, and others benefit. You also benefit from the medical records of everyone else, because trends and patterns emerge. Your medical records, for example, could be partnered with the medical record of someone half way around the world with the same identical medical history and condition.

For those readers concerned about privacy, we are moving into an economy and world where information becomes more transparent and available to all. It is not just that information becomes more available to all, that information must become available. To go back to our medical records example, it is simply not acceptable in our interconnected world to have someone with a contagious disease be able to conceal that information from society.

At the same time, laws will be enacted to prevent anyone or any entity from using that information in a way detrimental or harmful to you. Likewise, the learning data of every student will be protected so that information cannot be used to harm a student.

At this time learning data is in its infancy, if not prenatal condition. There is so little learning data available. Few learners have learning data records like we all have medical records. There is no ability to access learning records. The laws preventing misuse of learning data have yet to be enacted. And only a few people are studying and analyzing learning data.

Nevertheless, the experience with customer data, medical records, and online behavior tracking points to an exciting and emerging field of learning data, learning records, and learning data analysis.

We were talking with a limnologist living on the lake where we summer. He said he got started in limnology as a young person excited to pick up rocks and find craw daddies and other live creatures along the shore. Now, he said, he spends almost his entire day in front of a computer looking at Excel spreadsheet data about water clarity.

Our limnologist friend still walks the shore and still enjoys getting outdoors and on the lake. But he is more productive, and the taxpayers funding his work benefit more, when he is looking at Excel spreadsheet data. The reason: that's where the answers are.

A story in the *New York Times* on statisticians points to it as a growing new field with job opportunities for those with statistical analysis skills. While data analysis has always been a valuable activity, the immediate financial rewards and implications became clear with search engine optimization and other online economic analysis.

The *New York Times* story notes, "Traditionally, social sciences tracked people's behavior by interviewing or surveying them. 'But the web provides this amazing resource for observing how millions of people interact,' said Jon Kleinberg, a computer scientist and social networking researcher at Cornell."[15] The combination of software invention and return-on-investment of the analysis of the data produced are sure to make data analysis a critical component of numerous occupations and endeavors.

We only have a glimmer of how this will happen in education. But we do know it will happen. Here are some indications.

Tracking online interactions. There is now software that can and does track online behavior, plotting and graphing online interactions among people. By tracking interactions of people on Facebook and other social networks, certain patterns emerge. Students also learn by interacting with others online. Learning data software will be able to track online conversations and interaction, and then - based on one's own individual characteristics - suggest patterns of online interaction that will enhance the student's learning.

Predicting future likes. Netflix and other organizations are perfecting the algorithms and software to enhance the success of future choices based on one's past experience. As many people know, the online movie rental provider Netflix encourages people to rate movies they have rented. Then, based on the individual's ratings and preferences, Netflix is more likely to be able to predict and suggest other movies the individual might like. The system does not work perfectly, but it works in such a significant way that it is superior to other ways of judging movies, like movie reviews, box office sales, and testimonials.

So learning software will also ask learners to rate their experiences with games, readings, audio tapes as well as various kinds of content, and then also be able to assist learners in finding additional resources and ways of learning to enhance their academic achievement.

What we envision as happening is that software will be developed that will record both the learner's online activity and the learner's test scores, and then provide data for educators to analyze about the correlation and possible cause-and-effect of certain learning actions with better test scores. In-person behavior and activity will also be tracked, either using manual or software methods. Some possible learning data:

Online content interaction and test scores. When a particular student accesses online content, which forms of content delivery (text, audio, video, simulations, animations, pictures, etc.) are tied to better scores, and which combinations and lengths of time spent with each kind of content yield better scores?

Which behavior the student prefers. Which learning activities does the individual student prefer, and do those preferences lead to higher test scores?

Interpersonal interaction. With what kinds of mentors, peers and others does the individual student interact, what are the demographic or psychographic characteristics of those people, and which combinations and kinds of interaction help the individual student to learn more?

Rest time and breaks. How often should the student take a break, what kinds of non-learning activities (games, television, physical activity, shopping, play, jokes, cartoons, games, chat, food, naps) correlate to better test scores?

These are just some of the kinds of learning data that software will be able to retrieve and then match with test scores, giving the student, his or her parents, and teachers a better guide as to improving learning and maximizing the individual's time in learning.

But collecting the data will be the easy part. "But the big problem is going to be the ability of humans to use, analyze and make sense of the data" notes Erik Brynjolfsson, an economist and director of the Massachusetts Institute of Technology's Center for Digital Business. [16]

Teacher performance can also be analyzed by data analysis.[17] The data will find good and bad teachers of course. But beyond that, the data will also find that a poor teacher may actually excel with a certain kind of student, and that a very good teacher may not be able to help other kinds of students learn. This level of data analysis will maximize both learner and teacher performance.

The area of learning data is likely to become an entire specialty within education, with learning data analysts, software developers, and school and college specialists working with learners to interpret their own learning data. The emerging field of learning data will be a major way that enhances teaching, increases learning, and makes it possible to personalize learning for each student.

17. Teaching as a way of learning

In the factory model of schooling, students learn and teachers teach. But we know that one of the best ways to learn, possibly even the best way to learn, is to teach someone else.

One of the many virtues of the rural one-room schoolhouse of 100 years ago was that it integrated sharing and teaching as a way of learning. With students of all ages in one room, older students mentored and taught younger children.

Sharing one's knowledge with others actually enhances one's own knowledge.

Atul Gawande, writing in *The New Yorker* magazine, cites the story of the children's fibrosis hospitals in the United States. In the 1960s, a child might live one or two years after getting the disease, but not longer. Yet a doctor at a Cleveland hospital said his patients lived beyond the two years. This was causing unrealistic expectations and bad publicity for the other 39 hospitals in the country treating the disease. So the national organization sent a doctor from Minneapolis to Cleveland to hush up the outlandish claims of the doctor.

What the visiting doctor discovered was that indeed the Cleveland doctor's patients lived longer than the patients at the other hospitals. The national organization immediately asked the Cleveland doctor to train doctors at the other hospitals on his methods, and then began tracking life expectancy rates at all of the hospitals treating the disease.

After 40 years of sharing what worked, two things happened. As expected and hoped for, the life expectancy rates at all the other hospitals increased after the Cleveland doctor shared his expertise. What was not expected was a more startling result - the life expectancy rates of the Cleveland doctor's patients actually increased even more than those of the other hospitals. While every doctor and hospital benefited from the training, the Cleveland doctor doing the teaching actually benefitted more from the sharing than those being taught. The lesson: sharing one's expertise actually increases one's knowledge and expertise.[18]

18. Stage not Age

Moving from age to stage in student learning will be a major and welcome change in education. While it needs to occur in elementary and secondary education, its effects will extend to higher education, where the term "traditional" student still applies to the ages of 18-22, and "nontraditional" still refers to students over age 22.

We know all students do not learn at the rate and the same pace. We know young people mature at different rates and times. We know most people have differing abilities in different subjects. The idea that every student should and can be on page 72 in week seven is simply ridiculous, unsubstantiated by research and experience. It only exists because of the adherence to the factory model of education.

"The idea is that pupils' learning is built on and that they do not get bored by teachers repeating work they have already covered," notes a story on BBC Online. "The tailoring of lessons to the individual needs of pupils means they remain challenged by and interested in their work and that the pace of learning is kept up."[19]

As schools move from age to stage, curriculum can be tailored to the individual student, resulting in greater motivation, learning and teacher effectiveness.

19. Play is good

Play must be seen as a positive activity for students of all ages. At a minimum, play enhances and furthers learning. And play may very well be a prerequisite to learning.

For the past 100 years, however, educators have viewed play as wasteful and unproductive for all but the very young. The word "play" is most often viewed as a negative, while the word "work" is most often viewed as a positive. Educators frequently use such phrases as "Stop playing and get back to work."

In his 1920 book *Play in Education,* Joseph Lee wrote, "A great obstacle in interpreting the child to grown people is that we have no word which stands for the most important factor in the child's life. And the difficulty is enhanced by the fact that the word which we actually use to designate this factor has a significance almost diametrically opposed to the nature of the thing itself and helps continually to mislead us upon the subject. 'Play,' to grown people, signifies something of secondary importance: it is the word for those activities that must be postponed to serious pursuits. 'Child's play,' especially, means whatever is ridiculously easy. To the child, upon the other hand, play is the most important thing there is. It is primary, comes first, and represents real life; it is what all the rest is for. The most important play is play of the mind.

"And not only do we call the child's dearest interests by a name implying that they are of negligible importance, but we heighten the misunderstanding by (very properly) calling the same identical interests when they appear in grown people by a variety of high-sounding names, - such as work, art, science, patriotism, idealism, genius - that we never think of applying to children's play."[20]

Play, however, is a primary way in which young people discover their world and become aware of its wonderfulness, their potential, and the excitement of learning. The foremost educator of 100 years ago was G. Stanley Hall, president of Clark University and the first president of the American Psychological Association. He wrote that "In right play teaching, we are dealing in the very depths, and not the shallows, of the soul."[21] Lee noted, "The most important play is play of the mind."

In both our K-12 schools and our colleges and universities, play should be seen as a positive activity. "Play teaching," as Hall advocated for, remains a distant hope in instruction, but those teachers who engage in play teaching will certainly see the benefits for their students.

For example, The HighScope Preschool Curriculum Comparison Study found that children who learned mainly through playful activities fared much better at their work and social responsibilities than those in an academic instruction-oriented class.[22]

20. Rework is encouraged

In this century, rework will be encouraged and be a standard and accepted way of learning. Taking a test more than once, doing homework over a second time, revising an essay, and engaging in a project a second or even third time currently is not rewarded. Rework is frequently not even allowed. We know, however, that people learn by failure. We know that in this century the objective is not to compare one person to another, but to reach a benchmark. We know "practice makes perfect." In our schools and colleges rework must be common, normal, accepted and encouraged.

For example, Ontario, Canada "Teacher Joyce Wagland has always allowed students to hand in assignments late, as long as they finished the missing work in front of her. Wagland believes in second chances, which is why the former English department head signed on to be a credit-recovery teacher at an Ottawa high school. And she says a controversial provincial policy that gives students second chances at missed deadlines and tests solidifies something teachers have been doing for years. 'In the real world, if you make a mistake, you get a second chance,' she says. Credit recovery allows high school students who have acquired some of the necessary knowledge to redo the elements they missed and get their credit without taking the course all over again. It's part of a package of initiatives aimed at increasing Ontario's five-year graduation rate to 85 percent in two years from 68 percent five years ago. 'You can't give up on them when they're teenagers,' says high school principal Renald Cousineau. 'I see it as a moral imperative not to give up on students.'"[23]

21. Personalisation replaces the factory

Our 21st pedagogical concept and practice is that learning and teaching becomes personalised and customized to each individual student. We use the British spelling as educators in the United Kingdom first advanced the concept for education in this century.[24]

Personalisation is not just one approach or technique, it is the overarching and overall pedagogical strategy of this century, replacing the factory model of teaching and learning. It is the single foremost concept, goal and strategy for education and every teacher. Education and teaching becomes redesigned around personalisation and customization. Personalisation in teaching and helping our students to learn is what maximizes each student's learning potential. It is what makes it possible for each of our students to achieve. Personalisation of teaching allows each student to understand her or his skills, strengths and weaknesses. And in large measure it determines how each student can succeed in the workplace. It is the foundation and key to educational success and societal prosperity in this century.

Chapter 6.
Grading and Assessment: Tests Every Week

The system of grading and assessment of student learning that most institutions use today is the one created for the factory school of the last century.

The way learners are assessed in this century will be transformed and have these characteristics:

- Focused only on learning and knowledge.
- Objective, created by evaluation specialists, tested, and with cumulative data by different student demographic characteristics for benchmarking.
- Behavior, including time, attendance, work done and late work will not be considered.
- Multiple assessments will respond to differences in how we as individuals test.

The result will be that grading and assessment will not only more accurately reflect what a student has learned, but grading and assessment will become integrally part of the learning process.

There are a number of problems with the current system of grading and assessment. The problems include that the current system is:

- *Measuring inputs*. Time, work, timeliness, number of words and other inputs are measured rather than learning and knowledge outputs.
- *Subjective*. The current system is relying too much on teacher judgment and assessments that are not norm-referenced and tested.

- *One size fits all.* The current system is oriented towards the concept that one size fits all, with the same test administered to all students in a given class at the same time with no choice in test delivery options.
- *Behavior oriented.* Behavior unrelated to learning and knowledge, much of which is hard-wired and can arguably be attributed to neurology, is given too much weight in grades and assessment.

In the first two decades of the 20th century, the current system of grading and assessment was created largely in response to the need for education to prepare students for work and life in the factory and office.

The Carnegie Foundation took a leading role in the creation of time as a measurement of educational attainment. By 1910, nearly all secondary institutions in the United States used the "Carnegie Unit" as a measure of secondary course work.

The Carnegie Foundation contracted with Morris Llewellyn Cooke to explore ways to measure education at the higher education level. His resulting work, "Academic and Industrial Efficiency," was published in 1910 and became the basis for the Student Hour used by colleges and universities.[1]

Again, the motive here was to standardize educational measurement and faculty workloads. Cooke established the collegiate Student Hour as "an hour of lecture, of lab work, or of recitation room work, for a single pupil."

So the very foundation of education in the last century became a measure of time. One's educational attainment was largely measured by time, time as an input.

Grades also served the interests of the factory, and helped solidify the factory school model of the last century.

The grading system of A (excellent), B (good), C (average), D (below average) and F (failure) was based not on objective scores, but on a comparison with other students (sometimes referred to by students as "the curve").

This was helpful to the factory, where a major personnel issue was the assignment of people to various levels of jobs within the factory. Thus, a student who was a "C" student, and thus average, became a factory worker on the assembly line. A student who was a "B" student and above was more likely to be able to become a foreman or supervisor in the factory. And the "A" or excellent students went on to college and became the managers and professionals in the factory and office. In terms of high school education, by the 1920s society deemed a high school degree as essential for working in the factory, and made high school education "universal" with the goal of everyone graduating from high school.

In terms of college and university, society deemed that only around 25% of our nation's youth needed to be college graduates, and thus part of higher education's mission in the last century was to keep 75% of the youth out of college.

The resulting system, whether intentional or not, can arguably be said to have worked extremely well. Not only did the United States become the world's richest and most powerful nation, but the system was employed basically with the same tenets in other industrial societies around the world as well, boosting the standard of living for citizens in Europe, Russia, Japan, Australia and other industrialized nations.

The problems with the existing system of grading and assessment were virtues in the last century, when the most valuable work sector was the factory worker, and offices were run like factories. Consider:

- *Time inputs were the measure of productivity in the factory.* It is no coincidence that the tardy bell in high school rang in many schools at the same time as the factory whistle blew, signaling the start of the factory shift. Attendance and time put in were measured in the factory with time clocks, and attendance and time were what produced factory goods by the workers.

- *The teacher as evaluator of student achievement reflected the supervisor's role in the factory.* The supervisor evaluated workers. Teachers served as supervisors, the same function that foremen served in the factory and office supervisors or "middle management" served in the office.

- *One test or evaluation served all students, because in the factory all workers were, and had to be, the "same."* The factory was intentionally standardized with "one way" to produce goods in order to maximize efficiency. So students were preparing to work the same way, and be the same. Whether or not students were individuals or learned differently or tested differently was largely irrelevant to the needs of the factory.[2]

- *Behavior was integrally related to success and the productivity of the factory.* One could say that behavior was even more important than learning and knowledge in the factory or even the office. Attendance was essential, showing up on time critical, turning work in on time an absolute necessity, and behavior outside the acceptable norm simply inefficient and a hindrance to effectiveness of the factory and office.

In the knowledge work society of the post-industrial nations of the United States, Canada, Europe, Russia, Japan, Australia and others, none of the characteristics of the testing and assessment system of schools are relevant and of virtue today. Instead, they are all obsolete and either irrelevant or a hindrance to the most valuable work sector in the 21st century, the knowledge work sector.

Time input, in particular, is obsolete. We know now that attendance does not equal learning, and that someone sitting in a chair for eight hours does not necessarily learn more than someone sitting in a chair for four hours. We know that time is no longer a valid measurement of learning.

Less time is now valued more. The educational system of the last century had as a central tenet that the more time one put into one's education, the higher the level achieved. In this century, employers actually value the opposite. The sooner one learns something, the more quickly one achieves a level of knowledge, the more profitable for the company and the more productive the individual. So learning something in four hours is actually better in this century than learning the same amount of material in eight hours.

Even continuing education for workers today is based on an out-of-date system called Continuing Education Units, or CEUs. Spending 10 hours learning something qualifies for 1.0 CEU. Thus, if someone learns a given material in 5 hours, one is only rewarded with half the CEUs as the person who takes twice as long to learn the same material.

Complicating learning at the professional, higher education, and even elementary and secondary levels is that an increasing amount of learning is done online. Almost all colleges and universities have online classes available for their students. Online courses are increasing at the secondary level as well. But it is almost impossible to measure time spent learning online. Only a few agencies can measure time online with retinal scanners measuring eyeball time or fingerprints on the mouse pad. Even when that is feasible for educational institutions, it is still irrelevant to learning outcomes.

Teachers are awful at getting grades correct. Nancy S. Cole, at the time President of the Educational Testing Service, along with Warren Willingham determined that GPA (grade point average) was roughly equal to test score results for only about 45% of students (47% for females, 44% for males). (3) If we were grading teachers at grading, a 45% would be an "F," or failing.

Cole and Willingham document that some 28% of students get better grades than their test scores indicate they should receive, and that 28% of students get worse grades than their test scores indicate they should receive. We can debate whether giving a student a better grade than she or he deserved is worthwhile. There can be little debate about whether giving a student a worse grade than he or she deserves serves any purpose. Giving students worse grades than they deserve keeps too many of our smartest students out of college, prevents them from graduating from college, and thus creates a skilled worker shortage in some of our most valued profession such as science, engineering and technology, occupations critical to a knowledge economy in the 21st century.

Here we suggest that the way learners will be assessed in this century will be transformed to be:
- Focused only on learning and knowledge.
- Objective.
- Excluding behavior as a criterion.
- Employing multiple assessments.

Tests will be:

1. Benchmarked

The system to evolve will be composed of thousands of tests in thousands of different subject areas. Visually think of these tests as hurdles in a foot race.

The structure of knowledge in the 21st century is clearly towards units and subunits. So when a student has mastered a subunit or unit, she or he will take a test. If the student passes, that hurdle has been jumped and the student will move on to the next level.

Passing a test will no longer be based on a comparison with other student scores. In the knowledge society, one's work is judged by a standard or benchmark, irrespective of whether every other student passes or fails the same test.

For example, British, Canadian and American educators with the Commission on the International Learning Unit have proposed a testing and assessment standard called the International Learning Unit, or ILU. The benchmark for passing a test is 80%. If a student gets 80% of the questions correct, the student passes.[4]

Whether or not the International Learning Unit becomes the standard, some standard will be accepted by educational institutions for its validity, transferability, and ability to compare various tests and assessments.

2. Frequent

Instead of one test, or infrequent tests, testing will occur as frequently as the student wishes. When a student is prepared to take a test, she or he takes the test. This will be done as often as weekly.[5]

Re-testing. For most tests, retesting and taking the test over again will not only be allowed but encouraged. The idea is for everyone to pass, for everyone to learn good grammar, for everyone to spell correctly and do multiplication correctly.

Pre-tests. Pre-testing will become common, giving each student (and the student's teacher) a beginning measurement of learning and knowledge. From the pre-test, the student and teacher can determine how much the student has learned moving forward.

Quiz-outs. Students will be able to quiz-out on certain units and subunits simply by taking the test for that unit of material. In this way, students remain challenged and optimize the use of their time in studying material which is new.

3. Objective

Tests will be created by the best test-creation experts. They may be teachers, they may be testing experts. They may be amateurs, unpaid citizens with a particular excellence in a given subject or particular gift in test creation.[6]

Tests will be constantly evaluated, with data compiled in every way conceivable to provide feedback on relevance and reliability, as well as combining test scores with student demographics to show variances among different kinds of people.

4. Multiple assessment choices

If we learn differently, do we test differently? The correct answer is "Yes."

Thus, the word "test" is used here as an evaluation or assessment because it best conveys what the assessment accomplishes. But a "test" will not merely be a multiple choice, true or false, fill in the blanks kind of test. Those tests will be offered.

But these kinds of "tests" will also be available for each content

area:
- Essays and papers
- Oral exams
- Online comments
- Individual projects
- Group projects
- Practice or demonstration of skills (examples: taking blood for a nursing student; fixing a flat tire for a bicycle mechanic).
- Reflective journals
- Analysis of case studies
- Debates
- Role Plays
- Games
- Drag-and-drop exercises
- Gaming and virtual world demonstrations
- Physical construction of objects
- And others.

Tests will be constructed for different learning styles, such as the various learning styles of visual, kinetic, auditory, and sensory.

Tests will also be constructed to address various physical abilities and disabilities. Some students will choose to use blue pencils, sit in windowless rooms, have a lizard present, or take them at 3,000-foot elevations.

5. Given when ready

Tests will be given when the student is ready to take the test. As Mike Baker, Education Editor for *BBC News* writes, "Instead of preparing pupils for the high stakes tests at the end of each key stage, teachers' focus would be on assessing when a child is able to move up one level in the national curriculum grades. When they think a child is ready, they can put them in for a test that will be set and marked outside the school. They will not have to wait, as now, until pupils reach the end of a key stage at seven, 11 or 14. This will mean 'several shorter, more focused, and more appropriate tests' for each child, rather than one big test at the end of the key stage.[7]

6. Most tests online

Most tests will be taken online. But students who test best in-person, orally, or answering questions from a teacher, will also have those opportunities.

With online tests, creating, disseminating and evaluating a thousand tests in 10,000 subjects is both feasible and cost effective. With hundreds of millions of students in post-industrial countries taking the tests, there will be a sufficient sample for each kind of test from which to evaluate its relevance and effectiveness.

In summarizing grading and assessment for the 21st century, the way learners are assessed in this century will be transformed. Grading and assessment will be focused only on learning and knowledge. The new system of testing and assessment will be more objective, exclude behavior as a criterion, and employ multiple assessments. Pedagogically, best of all grading and assessment will become integrally part of the learning process. It won't just measure learning but actually enhance each student's learning.

Chapter 7.
Grading Learning, not Behavior: No Penalty for Late Work

An immediate problem in education is to eliminate grading based on behavior. All students should be graded solely on their learning and knowledge, not behavior. Grading based on behavior has detrimental effects for both female students and male students.

Currently grading is not based solely on learning and knowledge. Instead, grades are assigned to a great extent by behavior instead of learning and knowledge.

Graded behavior includes:
• Attendance in class.
• Coming to class on time.
• Turning homework and coursework in late.
• Not doing assigned homework or coursework.
• Taking exams and tests late.
• Other behavior deemed inappropriate by school authorities, including disagreements, acting out, clothing, chewing gum, bringing a pet to school, using a cell phone, etc.
• Out-of-school behavior, such as actions taken after school.
• Illegal behavior, including theft, downloading music, and destruction of property.

The role of schools and colleges in the 21st century is purely, entirely and totally about learning and knowledge, not about behavior.

There are no beneficial effects from including behavior in grading. The negative effects are numerous and troubling.

There are individual impacts. One student at Duke University was flunked simply for being on a sports team. That was the only reason. Because he was a senior, he could not graduate. His parents sued Duke University and the student was consequently allowed to graduate. Other students prevented from graduating based on their behavior are not so lucky.

In 2009 the University of Wisconsin Board of Regents passed a regulation allowing universities to discipline or even expel students for behavior outside the campus. If that rule were in place for Julie, she would not have been able to graduate from college. You see, she sat down at a lunch counter in the 1960s with African-Americans, which was against the law at the time.

These are extreme examples, but unfortunately they occur with too much frequency.

What happens every day in every school and in every college is that students are penalized for turning work in late, missing class, or not doing the work. This results in millions of students being prevented from entering or graduating from college, with disastrous consequences for society.

It means we tell students who know English and math that they do not know English and math, and it means we tell other students who do not know English and math that they do know English and math. It means that Grade Point Average (GPA) is not a measure of academic achievement. It instills the wrong values in our students.

One day a young man named Jason took a final exam in class. The teacher called him up to the front of the room and told him, "Jason, I've been teaching this class for 20 years, and no one has ever gotten all 200 questions correct. You got all 200 questions correct. Because you missed some classes, I'm giving you a 'C'."

The most outstanding American physicist of the 20th century, Robert Oppenheimer, was attending a university in Great Britain in 1925 when he tried to poison his instructor. The university put him on probation and ordered him to see a counselor. America and the world would have lost one of its most outstanding physicists if that university had expelled him based on behavior.

Grading based on behavior has disastrous consequences, grading based on learning and knowledge retains more of our best and brightest students.

Several million smart students are missing from college every year[1], consequently not graduating from college, and therefore not able to fill skilled knowledge work positions in the workforce. Others make it to college but do not graduate.

Implications for both male and female students

There are negative implications for penalizing students for behavior, such as late work, for both male and female students. Female students entering the workplace find that the behavior that was rewarded in school is not sufficient in the workplace. In school, a female student with good behavior can get a significantly higher grade than her learning and knowledge warrants. In the workplace, good behavior is far less important than productivity and profitability. In fact, female students learn five bad habits in school that hinder them in the workplace.

For male students, the impact is far more detrimental and immediate, for them, for the workplace, and for society. Males, especially boys and young men, get worse grades than females, especially girls and young women. The lower GPAs among male students keep about 2 million smart boys out of college every year. These male students test at or above the level of females admitted to college.

Consequences for society

As a result, there are now shortages of scientists, engineers, computer scientists and others at a time when knowledge workers are needed to ensure prosperity in the new century for post-industrial nations such as the United States, Canada, UK and others.[2]

There is such a shortage of veterinarians that USA Today recently said that it "threatens" our food supply.[3] Overall, there is a serious shortage of knowledge workers.

A shortage of college graduates means the country is at a disadvantage in global competitiveness. The United States and Canada, for example, do not graduate nearly the number of college graduates necessary for the knowledge society of the 21st century, while other countries have set goals, such as the United Kingdom's (England) goal for 50% of its citizens to be college graduates.

There are issues with saying an underachieving student is a high-achieving student. But there are even more serious consequences of saying that a high-achieving student is an underachieving student. It means that many high-achieving students, predominantly male, don't just get poor grades. More critically, they also have a lower retention rate and lower graduation rate. This is why male students have been a minority of college graduates for 30 years and are less than 40% of college graduates.

As a result, society has a shortage of college-educated youth. We can quantify that shortage. Estimates of the national shortage run as high as 14 million skilled workers by 2020, according to widely cited projections by the labor economists Anthony P. Carnevale and Donna M. Desrochers.

US Department of Education data indicate that a significant portion of smart students get lower grades than their learning and knowledge scores indicate (4). Studying the issue for the past ten years, we have discovered that one of the primary reasons why smart students are not entering college in sufficient numbers, and not graduating from college in sufficient numbers, is that teachers and faculty penalize students for late work, including homework and coursework.[5]

Other educational experts (e.g. Harris Cooper) have shown there is no relationship between completing homework and test scores.

The Toronto School Board District in 2008 approved a policy prohibiting teachers from penalizing students for late homework, with "progressive" penalties for late coursework.[6]

Grades don't measure what students know

"Grades…. are often not accurate measures of what students know," writes Dr. John Woodward, Director of Research and Development for the NCA Commission on Accreditation and School Improvement. He writes, "In theory grades could be one of the best indicators of student learning, if certain conditions were met. However, in practice, teachers include many factors that are not related to what students know when grading those students."[7]

The numbers

In comparing grades and test scores, Educational Testing Service researchers Warren Willingham and Nancy Cole[8] found:

	Boys	Girls
Grades and test scores roughly the same	44%	47%
Grades are significantly better than test scores	20%	33%
Test scores are significantly better than grades	36%*	20%*

* This is where the problem is.

For a significant portion of the student population, the students test much higher than their grades. The primary reason they receive lower grades is they are penalized for late work. This keeps them from either entering or graduating from college. The problem is now affecting a growing number of smart girls. The rate of growth of dissatisfaction with school is now higher among girls than among boys. Coates' interview with a psychologist indicates that he is seeing the consequences of this dissatisfaction among girls at a much higher rate now than in the past.

Late students test just as well

Studies confirm that the group most penalized for late work scores about the same on a variety of tests as other students, including the ACT, SAT, and College Board Advanced Placement exams.

Homework is the problem

An important study is one done by the Edina, Minnesota, public schools. It is important in these respects:

1. It pinpoints homework as the determining factor in the GPA gap.
2. The study reports on numerous testing measures, showing that boys and girls score roughly the same on a variety of tests.
3. The study is comprehensive in nature, providing data from a single school district that both correlates with national data, and shows clearly the relationships with a specific case study.[9]

The link between homework and grades

Since homework constitutes a significant factor in Grade Point Average (GPA), it is not surprising that Harris Cooper, a leading researcher on homework, reports that "The correlation between time spent on homework and class grades was +.47 for Tonglet (2000) and +.21 for Cooper et al. (1998)."[10] What this means is that homework scores are a primary factor as to why some students get lower grades than others.

No link between homework and tests

Dr. Cooper also reports no significant correlation (+.07) between time spent on homework and standardized achievement test scores, noting "No strong evidence was found for an association between the homework-achievement link and the outcome measure (grades versus standardized tests) or the subject matter (reading versus math)."

The Solution Works

Woodward supports the contention that grades should not be based on behavior unrelated to learning and knowledge, recommending:
1. Grades should not be based upon attendance, punctuality, or behavior in class.
2. Grades should not be used to reward or to punish students. The purpose of the grade is to represent what students have learned.
3. Homework completion should not be a part of the grade. For many reasons homework completion is not an indicator of what was learned.

In 2009 we received the first evidence that the solution works. A high school teacher in Florida sent us the grades for her 100 students by sex. Male students had a GPA of 3.02 while female students had a GPA of 3.08, no significant difference.

We hope that more studies are done to illustrate that the solution works.

Eventually, all teachers will be prohibited by law from grading based on behavior.

Faculty objections

Teachers almost always give two reasons for penalizing students for late work:

"We're teaching responsibility."

There is no evidence to support this claim. In a survey we conducted of teachers, 84% said boys more often turn in work late. Only 4% said girls more often turn in work late; some 8% said neither sex turns in work late more often than the other; and the other 4% said they do not know. So turning homework in late is clearly a behavior that is more characteristic of male students than female students.

If teachers answered either girls or boys, they were then asked if turning homework in on time would improve (help) their grade. 96% of teachers replied 'Yes' and only 4% said 'No.'

Since almost all teachers penalize students for late work, if teachers were indeed teaching responsibility, then the GPA gender gap would close over a period of time. But the gender GPA gap never closes. That is, the so-called "responsibility" is never gained.

There is a gender GPA gap starting as early as sixth grade, and the gender GPA gap never closes, not even for seniors in college, where male students (the most responsible of all males) still get worse grades than female seniors.

So penalizing students for late work never has the intended consequence of teaching them "responsibility."

"We're preparing students for the workplace."
There is no evidence to support this claim either. While workers do have to turn work in on time in the workplace, there is no gender problem in the workplace with regard to turning work in on time. If indeed penalizing students for behavior had an impact on their performance in the workplace, then we would see females showing up more on time and turning their work in on time as compared to males in the workplace.

However, there is no gender difference in showing up on time and submitting work on time. Young men, including boys, show up at work on time and submit work on time just as often and frequently as young women.

Clearly employers report that some of their employees show up late for work or complete their work late. But there is no evidence in any studies that those late workers are the same people as the students who turn in school work late.

We have found no studies that young men perform more poorly than young women in the workplace. We have interviewed human resource professionals, and they indicate there is no problem. There is no perceived problem of boys in the workforce on the part of employers, workers or even educators.

We have not found any citations or references on the web as to any gender differences at work. We are only able to document evidence that women perform at the same level in the workplace as men, and most commentary on workplace gender issues tries to confirm that women perform up to men in the workplace.

In addition, we asked human resource executives if there is a problem of either gender showing up for work late or submitting work late. No human resource executive has documented any problem. We interviewed staff at two human resources associations and the president of a national employment agency.[11]

Some educators have told us that boys who simultaneously are enrolled in school and have part-time jobs show up on time for work and turn in homework late. Thus, there is no problem in the workplace, only in academia.

In the workplace, "responsibility" does not appear to be an issue in hiring. The problem is not that there are no responsible engineers or computer scientists, the problem is that there are not enough skilled (college-educated) engineers and computer scientists.

No change in on-time work

From interviews with teachers who currently do not penalize students for late work, they report that most students still turn in homework and coursework on time[12], and that the pattern of lateness does not change regardless of whether there is a penalty or not. Thus, there is no evidence that most students will regularly turn in work late. Instead, the evidence suggests that if the work is due on Friday, the same majority of students will turn the work in by Friday.

Incomplete policy not affected

Teachers currently have an "Incomplete" option for work not yet turned in. Work not turned in can still be tagged "Incomplete" until it is turned in.

Teachers can change

Clearly, the pedagogy of the 21st century does, and will continue to, demand that teachers treat learners as individuals, responding to them in individual ways that maximize the learning and knowledge of each one of them. The Internet provides the technology for instructors to be able to record individual progress and increasingly personalize teaching for each student. Accepting late work will not increase teacher workload in any significant way.

The Historical Parallel

For students being penalized for lateness, the punishment is very much like hitting students 100 years ago. Some 100 years ago, good teachers hit their students. Good fathers hit their children. Hitting a child was believed to instill moral character. It was also believed to be a motivation for better behavior.

In the first "talking movie picture" in the United States, *The Jazz-singer,* made in 1927, the jazzsinger Al Jolson as a child is punished for singing secular rather than solely religious music. Even when the child threatened to run away from home, his father whipped him one more time. His father, a religious man, believed he was being a good father by whipping his son.

The problem was that hitting students had absolutely no positive effect on learning, motivation, or even behavior. Instead, millions of children dropped out of school. When the social worker Julia Johnson interviewed 800 children who had dropped out of school, the primary reason why they would not return to school was that the teacher hit them.[13]

As education became transformed to meet the needs of the industrial age, state laws became enacted to outlaw hitting students, eventually affecting schools in most states in America.

What hitting did to students was at least as or more emotional in nature than physical. The student was labeled "bad" when he or she was hit. Today students are labeled as "bad" for lateness. The negative self-esteem, combined with the humiliation from others, is devastating for many students, and we again have millions of so-called drop-outs today for very much the same reason.

Teachers today are under the mistaken impression that behavior is totally willful. Instead much behavior is based on one's neurology, hormonal composition, physical disability, brain development or other hard-wired and natural cause. Punishment does not help an individual to change his or her neural abilities.

And behavior is irrelevant to learning and knowledge. Teachers, schools and colleges should not measure or correlate behavior with learning and knowledge.

Way too much time and resources are spent by teachers, schools and colleges in trying to manage, change, measure, judge and punish behavior. This valuable time takes away from actually helping individuals to learn.

To further the argument, the National Center for Education Statistics also provides data that teachers focus on behavior way too much. According to the NCES of teachers, teachers themselves report that they feel most capable in managing behavior in the classroom. So this is the skill set that most teachers are most proud about. And the skill set that most teachers feel the weakest is that related to technology and the Internet.

Teachers in the early part of the 21st century have their priorities reversed. They are least skilled in the technology of the Internet, the area that has the most potential and capability of helping students learn in this century. And they say they are most skilled in managing behavior, the area that is the most irrelevant in helping students to learn.

Some Illustrations
Punishment Did Not Work

Julie Jorgenson is an executive from Minnetonka, Minnesota. Her child turned in homework late. And grades suffered for it. She and her husband agreed to punish the child by taking something out of the child's bedroom every time homework was turned in late. Within a month the only items left in the child's bedroom were the bed and books. The parents agreed it was counterproductive to take the books out of the bedroom.

The next semester Mrs. Jorgenson negotiated with the child's teachers to guarantee that if there was no penalty for late work, she would guarantee the homework would be turned in within a reasonable period of time, usually less than a week after the due date. The teachers agreed, and the child's grades skyrocketed.

Emotional Damage and Hurt

We interviewed Langdon Divers, who was 102 at the time of the interview. Mr. Divers, a successful businessman and professor, related that when he was a senior in high school he was the only student in his class to pass his physics exam. All the other students flunked physics. However, because he turned in his workbook late, Mr. Divers was flunked by his teacher and all the other students were passed. Because he was a senior in high school, Mr. Divers had to take the whole senior year over again, even all the classes he had passed. The emotional damage and hurt caused by this was clear 85 years later as Mr. Divers understated, "He didn't handle it very well, did he?"

Testing Above Average

Kentaro Takahashi was an AFS student from Japan. Some 10,000 Japanese high school students applied to become AFS students in the United States. Kentaro was one of only 100 Japanese students accepted. After completing high school in the United States, he got a job with a New York magazine. He took his SAT exam for university, getting a 1250, about 250 points higher than the average American student scores on the SAT. He took the SAT in a foreign language (English). However, because he turned his school work in late in high school, he was given a 2.0 GPA. Despite the fact that he was talented and brilliant, there was no university in the entire United States that would accept him as a student.

Attendance Required

Shaina Humphreys was an "A" student throughout high school. However, in her senior year, she contracted a disease where she had to stay home for most of her final semester under doctor's orders. She turned in all her assignments, getting an "A" on her final essay. However, because she was not able to attend class, she was flunked and prohibited from graduating for her absent behavior, even though she passed all the knowledge requirements. That is, she was graded based on her behavior rather than on her knowledge.

Getting All the Problems Correct

Tristan Wiley, a young African American, had 30 math homework problems. He turned in 10. He got all 10 problems correct. His grade? F of course. So Tristan got every problem correct, and got an F. His teacher told his mother, his school and any prospective colleges that Tristan did not know math. Tristan knew he knew his math.

Taking the Test Late

Lynn Mack is an instructor at Piedmont Technical College in South Carolina. A young African American student failed to show up for the final exam in a math class she was teaching. But she really wanted the student to pass the course, so she took the exam to the college testing center and said that if he showed up within a week, to give him the test. Two weeks later he showed up. But Lynn Mack really wanted him to pass the course, so she told the testing center to just give him the exam. He scored a 97. Most teachers would have flunked this smart student, preventing him from obtaining a college education and a likely good job contributing to the knowledge economy. Most teachers would have been content to send him to McDonald's or Walmart.

Why Teachers Teach "Responsibility"

We were driving in northern Wisconsin one day when our car broke down, and we barely made it to the Little Star Garage in Manitowish Waters to have it repaired. Started way back in the 1950s, the repair shop still had a pit instead of a car lift, a hole in the garage where the mechanic walks down underneath the car. When we went to pay, we noticed this quotation on the pricing board, "To educate a man in mind and not morals is to educate a menace to society, Theodore Roosevelt." It suddenly became clear to us why teachers teach "responsibility" in schools and college.

When Theodore Roosevelt wrote that quotation, the United States was in the last stages of being an agrarian society, one in which half of the population lived on family farms. The rural and small town society, in which people rarely travelled more than eleven miles away from home, was such that morality and moral character were essential social mores to the success of rural and small town civilization.

So teachers in the one-room rural schoolhouses taught morality and moral character. But they did not teach what you and I would regard as morality or moral character. They did not mean just vague and broad values like not stealing or not lying, virtues throughout the ages. By morality and moral character they also meant specific kinds of behavior for those times. They taught behaviors that, once again, were essential to the success of rural and small town society.

Going outside without a hat on, moving away more than eleven miles, putting your parents in a home for the elderly, driving or shopping or working on Sunday, not standing by your oral word - these were all immoral behaviors not to be engaged by anyone with moral character. They were behaviors that you and we engage in all the time and do not see as wrong. By the standards of your great-great grandmother, you and we are immoral.

Let us illustrate. Julie's grandfather once bought 300 acres on which to farm. He found a place down by the creek that was the best place to build his house. Then he invited his brother to locate his house anywhere he liked on the farm. His brother, knowing Julie's grandfather had picked out the best spot down by the creek, said he wanted the spot down by the creek. Julie's grandfather - unwilling to go back on his word, not wanting to be seen in the community as someone not honoring his word, wanting to uphold his moral character - allowed his brother the spot down by the creek for his house.

That is moral character. That is something that few of us would do today. But in order to maintain relations in business and in community life back then, it was necessary to honor one's word. Not as many people could write, lawyers were fewer and more expensive, and business was conducted with neighbors one saw almost every week. Social cohesion demanded honoring one's word.

And so parents and teachers taught morals and moral character, hitting their children and students to help instill moral character in them. A good parent, a good teacher, was a person who hit children. We know now that hitting students does not instill moral character, nor

90

anything else beneficial. We know that 100 years ago hitting students caused millions of them to drop out of school and work in the newly created factories where they did not get hit. We now have laws in most states and most post-industrial nations against hitting students in school.

Likewise, teachers today, in the last stages of the Industrial Age, teach "responsibility." And by responsibility teachers mean certain and specific behaviors, including showing up, showing up on time, doing the work, and turning work in on time.

Instructors teach "responsibility" because the specific behaviors meant by "responsibility" were essential to work in the factory and the office of the last century. Teachers do not teach the morality and moral character that the teachers of 100 years ago taught, because those behaviors became obsolete. In fact, in the last century it was a sign of success to move more than eleven miles away from home, getting the promotion and big job at the corporate headquarters. In living 100 years ago, there was "no place like home," but in the 20th century a good person was someone with "get up and go," a "go getter," the opposite value of the agrarian age.

Likewise, the smartest students of today will become - must become - knowledge workers, not factory or office workers. They will work not in an office but in whatever location and environment allows them to be most productive and most profitable for their company or employer. They will not need to show up on time, because their employers will want them to work at their own peak work time, not on a factory or office 8-5 schedule. They will be paid not by time input but by productivity output. They will get more pay for doing something in less time, not more time.

Just as you and I are not moral in the sense that our teachers meant 100 years ago, so your students are not and will not need to be "responsible" in the obsolete meaning of the factory and office of the Industrial Age.

Teaching students to show up at 8 a.m. is just as obsolete as teaching them not to move more than eleven miles away from home.

It is not that morality and responsibility will disappear or be considered irrelevant in this century. There are likely to emerge other kinds of meaning to morality, moral character and responsibility. It is just that adults born in the last century do not know what values should look like in the Information Age of this century.

For example, at the time of this writing, most adults would argue that downloading a copyrighted movie is "piracy," immoral and should remain illegal. Your students understand that downloading multimedia such as movies is an absolutely essential economic activity for any knowledge worker, and must be considered both moral and legal. Even as a different set of values emerges, and morality and responsibility get redefined, we must not confuse behavior with learning and knowledge.

Assessing learning and knowledge, not behavior, is the proper concern of teachers, schools and colleges in the 21st century.

Grading on the basis of behavior no longer has any function in our schools and higher education. Instead, it has created a distorted and dysfunctional assessment of student learning and knowledge that is harming students, society and the workplace. It also is the source of an enormous waste of educational resources in terms of teacher and administrative time, time that schools cannot afford to waste. The elimination of grading on the basis of behavior is essential in properly assessing a student's actual learning and knowledge. In this century, the proper assessment of a student's learning is a critical precondition to helping that student learn more, graduating our smartest students from college, and preparing the most qualified workforce for our society.

Chapter 8.
The Pedagogy of Trains:
How Trains Change Education

Transportation has always had an important role in shaping education, schools and colleges. In the last century, the dominance of the automobile led to "commuter" campuses. The auto also created suburbs and contributed to consolidated school districts, thus causing many students to take a bus to school. Before 1920, most people walked or took the dominant transportation, the horse and wagon (or buggy or carriage). Both modes essentially had speeds of three miles an hour, causing one-room schoolhouses to be built every 3-6 miles apart (depending on the area of the country), within an hour's walk for the average child and farm family.

Trains will undoubtedly drastically alter not just how students get to school and college, but also how schools and colleges are designed and how education is delivered.

Trains and schools

Trains and light rail will have a profound effect on elementary and secondary schools. With a majority of people living in urban areas, and a majority of urban areas being served by light rail and trains, the change in transportation will impact most children in society.

Trains are the new school buses

For elementary and secondary schools, trains are the new school buses of the 21st century.[1] The consolidated school district of the last century arguably would not have been possible if it were not for school buses. In 2008, for example, 55% of the nation's school children took a school bus to school.[2]

High schools are almost intentionally built to be too far away for most students to walk to, further leading to obesity in children.

Communities are becoming denser.[3] Dense middle-class neighborhoods in the 21st century will be far safer than even middle-class suburban neighborhoods of the last century. That's because in the middle-class suburban neighborhood there are few people in the street, fewer eyes and ears open. People are driving to work or school, emptying out suburban neighborhoods during the day. Most places are way too far away to walk to. There is a reluctance to let children out in the middle-class suburb neighborhood for fear of "stranger danger," that someone will abduct one's child, even though the statistics indicate that most child abductions are done by family members or friends, not strangers. Even so, the rate of child abductions has fallen over the two decades from 1990 to 2010, according to the co-founder of "No child left inside."[4]

In dense middle-class neighborhoods, there will be much less to little risk in sending one's child on a train to school. There will be too many people all around in the streets, almost every child will have a cell phone, and there will be web cams and video cameras in most public places.

Kentaro Takahashi from Toyko came to live with us while he was a student in high school. We asked him how old he was when he first took a train by himself. He replied six, taking the train to school. We asked him where his parents were when he was taking the train to school. He just looked a little incredulous at us and replied, "They were working of course." We asked him how old he was when he first took a train out of the city to another city. He replied six.

Choosing schools

With many people living in dense communities less than a mile from a light rail or high-speed train station, it is possible for an elementary school-age child to attend a school 100 miles away (less than an hour travel time) and come home every day after school. A parent might want to send a child to a school 100 miles away because it specializes in meeting the needs of that child. It might be a school for Catholics, Lutherans or Muslims. It might be a school for children with Asperger's. It might be a school for those gifted in art. It might be a school where classes are offered in Spanish as well as English. It might be a school that maintains Somali culture, or that of the Ojibwa. So schools will become more niched and more differentiated, responding to specific learning needs of individuals rather than being factory schools that look alike and provide the same content, format and have the same rules and procedures.

More resources

They say this is the first century in which there are more educational resources outside of the school building than inside it. With light rail and trains, students can travel safely to access resources outside of school. That might be a museum, a state capitol, a college class, a botanic garden, a business, or any number of other resources that both provide information and stimulate learning.

Back and forth from home

With the school bus, there is just one opportunity to go to school, and one time to go home. And of course the entire school starts at just one time, and ends at just one time. With light rail and trains that run multiple times during the day, it is possible for a student to go back and forth during the same day from home and school.

In a school which responds to a person's peak learning time and needs to be utilized eighteen hours a day, there is no one start time for school anyway. So students can arrive at various times of the day, and depart at various times of the day. As children get older and more mature, they will also be allowed to come to school for a class, and then go home during the day, maybe even come back later for another class. All of this enables schools to maximize space, teachers, and individual attention for students.

Study while travelling

Children are able to study while travelling. So travel time no longer is wasted time. Learning does not start at school. Learning takes place at home, in school, and while on light rail or trains.

Field trips

The classic field trip is just as vital and important and stimulating in this century. Only a field trip on a high-speed train can now involve travelling hundreds of miles and back in a single day to see events, festivals, lectures, zoos, aquariums, and meet with any number of interesting people.

Triple the school resources

One huge advantage of light rail and trains on pedagogy for schools is that each school no longer has to have the same facilities. In the current factory school model, every school has the same facilities, staffed and resourced at the same level. So there is an art room, a chemistry lab, a music room, and a physics lab.

In the specialized, niched and operationally consolidated school system of this century, not every school needs a chemistry lab. Instead, students can travel to the school with the chemistry lab. The advantage for the student is that the centralized chemistry lab will be state-of-the-art, with far more resources and equipment than if every school needed the same equipment. And the centralized chemistry lab will have far more expert faculty. Because schools will be open eighteen hours a day, the chemistry lab is then used eighteen hours a day, three times longer than a typical chemistry lab in a factory model school. This allows school systems to triple the school resources for the same number of students, achieving both increased learning and budgetary savings.

Trains and colleges

For higher education, there are similar issues and opportunities in planning for trains, with some distinctions and differences. The issues for higher education do not include the effect on students, but the effect on faculty and administrators.

Campus location

The most obvious issue is whether or not a given college campus is on a train line. If a campus is not on a train line, the majority of students will not be able to get to the campus. There will be some campuses that intentionally remain off train lines, and some students will value the uniqueness of the college (for example, a religious college or fine arts institution) to such an extent that they will spend the extra time and resources required to get there. But the majority of students, given the choice of a campus on a train line and one off the train line, will choose the campus or campuses on train lines.

One basic reason is that the majority of college students beginning in 2020 will not own cars.[5] It is even unclear whether after 2030 most students will even know how to drive. We know this because it happened once before, 100 years ago. Almost every child knew how to ride a horse and drive a cart, up until the invention of the automobile. Then the percentage of children with riding and wagon-driving skills declined. Alice Draves, born in 1920, remembers her father urging her to learn how to ride a horse "just in case," as he put. Julie, growing up in the mountains, learned how to ride a pony as a young girl and actually did encounter a "just in case" circumstance in which she had to ride her horse to get a doctor. But for most people growing up after 1920, there was no need to learn how to ride a horse.

Generation Y, born 1980-1999, is the first generation to not only drive less but to stop buying cars. Gen Y, which is the first knowledge worker generation to earn its living primarily with intangible products, does not value tangible or material goods in and of themselves. "Shop until you drop" will probably not be a slogan your grandchildren will recognize. Gen Y views material goods on a scale of inconvenient to destructive of the environment. The less material goods, the better. Financially, cars are too expensive. In 2010 dollars, cars cost around $30 a day ($10,000 a year divided by 365 days) just to sit in a garage. And that does not include the cost of the garage. By comparison, in 2010 it cost only $8 an hour to rent a ZipCar, and just $20 a day to rent a U-Haul van.

So campuses not on train lines will simply be too difficult to get to for the typical college student.

The obsolete campus

Every action taken before January 1, 2020, to position your institution for the 21st century will have an exponential positive impact after Jan 1, 2020. Institutions not repositioning themselves will decline in both perceived and real value after January 1, 2020, at a rate of about 1% a month, so that by the year 2030 most all institutions not repositioned for the 21st century will essentially be worthless as an entity, and will be "sold for parts." Some institutions will exist beyond 2030 as Industrial Age institutions, but they will decline in number, just like one-room schoolhouses continued throughout the 20th century, until there were just a handful of them in 2000.

Campuses not on train lines can take these actions, in order of priority and preference:

• Get on a train line. Advocate for a train line to come to your city and campus.
• Create shuttle service. Create a shuttle service, such as bus service, to meet every train at the nearest station and take people to and from campus.

- Develop a satellite campus. Develop or expand one or more satellite campuses that are on train lines.
- Become totally virtual or online institution. Convert all of your classes to online.
- Integrate the campus into the community. Buy or rent buildings all over the community, making the community the campus. The Savannah College of Art and Design (SCAD) in Savannah, Georgia, is an excellent model for integrating the campus into the community.

The brick and mortar campus

And then there will be about a quarter of institutions that fail to change at all. Most of them will go into decline. There will be a race to the bottom, with too many institutions claiming they want to serve the traditional age student in the traditional classroom at the traditional campus. Like the decline of the one-room schoolhouse, these institutions will compete to be the last brick and mortar campus, a downward competition that will take many decades to decide. What we know is that almost all colleges and universities have to be transformed or risk being shuttered. The advantages of any college or university in this century are technology and faculty. Buildings are a cost, a weakness, a disadvantage, not a strength. Technology and faculty can be moved overnight.

Systems have the edge.

At the state/provincial or regional level, systems of institutions will become the effective functioning delivery mode. Only systems will have the critical mass of resources to respond to the individual needs of students. It is simply too cost prohibitive, and lacking in quality, for a campus or 20th century traditional institution to be able to respond quality-wise, subject-wise, operations-wise, to the needs of students, the community and society.

College and university campuses on train lines can become part of one system and thrive providing these services and activities.

Students move to other institutions for individual classes.

Students will be able to take the train and go to other campuses for one or more classes. With hybrid classes, it will be common for classes to meet only once or twice a week, so students won't be spending their entire days on trains. Of course, while on the train they can study.

Recruitment is more advantageous.

Recruitment of students is more advantageous for at least two reasons. The first is that the student can live at home, or wherever she or he wants, and still get to campus on the train every day and be able to return home at night. The second advantage is that campuses in a system will have more resources, choice of courses and available professors than a single campus.

Specialized, niche subjects are offered.

Having more courses, faculty and students means that the campuses or institutions participating in the system can define themselves more. They can establish an image and uniqueness by offering more specialized, advanced and niche subjects. From these offerings the institutions gain more recognition, more academic standing, and can recruit more of the best students from all over the world.

Outstanding specialties are highlighted.

As a result of having the ability to have more specialized and niche subjects, institutions can choose to have one or a few outstanding specialties, each becoming one of the foremost institutions in the world in a given specialty or subspecialty.

Faculty recruitment is more advantageous.

Just as campuses on train lines in a system have an advantage in recruiting students, they also will have an advantage in recruiting and retaining faculty. Like students, faculty can live elsewhere and take the train to work. And having more resources and specialties also gives faculty a greater opportunity to become specialists, teach niche and advanced courses, engage in research and take advantage of the greater resources.

Pedagogical impact of trains

The impact of trains extends beyond distance and travel, changing the pedagogy of the 21st century.

Because of trains, schools and especially colleges and universities will of necessity have to change the way in which curriculum is offered. The speed and safety of trains means that campuses and schools located 100 miles away are now only an hour away, the equivalent of the time it takes a child ten miles away from a high school to get there by school bus.

One of the biggest pedagogical changes is that students will be able not only study on trains, because the ride is quieter, safer for laptops and experiences fewer bumps and disruptions. But they will also be able to log onto the Internet and actually "be in class" in the online classroom, discussing online with their teachers and fellow students. Here are some of the other ways in which pedagogy is changed by trains.

Place becomes less important.

The need to identify place disappears. In the late 1990s, when we had an office, we had a staff member who would often call in on her cell phone, almost always beginning the conversation "I'm in Burnsville now." It became a small joke, but as the first decade of the new century wore on, people less and less identified where they were when they called. Today, our techie, who lives in Minnesota, will call in with normal business conversation, ignoring totally any need to explain that he is in Utah at that particular moment.

The New Yorker ran a classic cartoon around the same time showing three people on cell phones on a subway train. The first says, "I'm getting on the train now." The second says, "I'm on the train now." And the third person says into his cell phone, "I'm getting off the train now."

Time is redefined.

The second, and one of the most profound, changes that trains make in education, is that it is quite debatable, and maybe impossible to determine, whether it takes an hour for someone to travel by train 100 miles. Does it really "take an hour" if one is working all of the time? In 2010 transportation officials were measuring the time new high-speed trains would take to get from one city to another by comparing the time to travel by car between the same two cities. But if one can walk to the train station and get on a train in 10 minutes, and then walk 10 minutes to a school, campus or building after getting off the train 200 miles away, does it really take 2 hours and 20 minutes in travel time, or does it in 21st century reality take only 20 minutes (walking time), the person having been working or studying for the 2 hours while on the train.

This is a game-changer for education. Because then travel does not "take time." Students studying on the train and faculty logged into online discussion boards means that travel time is essentially irrelevant, and that a faculty member can teach at an institution 200 miles away and return home each evening with almost no "commute" time. Students can take one class at one location, get on a train and go to their next class 150 miles away, and have the travel take no time at all, studying all the way, making the class 150 miles away as convenient and close as a classroom next door - as if the classrooms were located next to each other in the same building.

We emailed the chancellor of a university in a statewide system, telling him of our work on the implications of a new high-speed train for higher education in his state. "Yes," he happily emailed back, "I'll be able to take the train to the capital for my meetings."

What the chancellor apparently did not realize is that his students can also take the train to the capital city and, once bureaucratic red tape gets cut, take classes on the campus of another university in the system in the capital city.

The bureaucratic red tape will get cut, as students demand and eventually force administrations to allow students to take classes on different campuses. Enlightened administrations may actually be pro-active and encourage cross-campus class-taking, understanding that increased quality of education that can be provided while at the same time reducing costs.

Faculty teach at multiple campuses.

The third implication is that faculty will find it much easier to teach at more than one institution, provided they are located in cities on train lines. Whether for an adjunct faculty member or a full-time faculty member, campuses within the same system of higher education will have the opportunity to share a particular faculty member. Alliances outside of systems, much like athletic conferences, will likely be formed to share faculty members as well.

Curriculum is redefined

The curriculum becomes redefined on a system or multiple-campus basis in a number of different ways.

Specialty faculty developed.

Outstanding high-quality professors and departments will be grown, cultured and nurtured on one particular campus, with other campuses de-emphasizing or even eliminating courses or departments, sending their students to the other campus for the subject matter.

The 'we serve everyone' university is dead, a product of the last century where automobile transportation and the pyramid did not allow students to engage in taking courses at multiple campuses - and where the curriculum was an extension of the quadrivium, essentially creating "general education" courses that all colleges took before being able to enter a major area of study. Even the majors were limited to a couple of dozen disciplines or so. The reason is that higher education was preparing millions of students for dozens of jobs, unlike this century when colleges must prepare dozens of students for their choice of millions of jobs.

So there are two Industrial Age higher education features that will collapse in the new train environment. The first is the need to have the same general areas of study in each university, since students were limited by the automobile (as well as other features of life in the 20th century) and could not reasonably travel from one campus to another. So every university had psychology, sociology, biology, English and so on.

The second Industrial Age feature was that higher education was preparing millions of people for dozens of jobs. This was a very different mission than the 21st century mandate of preparing dozens of people for millions of jobs. One can quibble over the exactness of those two quantifications, but the general difference is undoubtedly significant and real.

As an aside, this is one reason why many working adults today have a hard time telling their parents what they do for a living, because the specialization and fragmentation of the job market is proceeding at such a rapid pace. At the height of the last century, around 1960, lawyers were lawyers and doctors were doctors. There was some specialization, but not a lot. Today of course there is far more specialization, not just in law and medicine, but in every field.

Courses that have too few students for a given campus can be consolidated.

If there are not enough students for a Japanese language course or 16th Century French poetry course on a given campus, the students can travel to another campus. Many subjects that currently are not offered on any one campus will be able to be offered in the face-to-face format as well as online.

Courses will have 100 or more students in them, again.

Educational studies show that the quality of the teacher is the most important indicator of learning success for a student.

In an ideal world, we would all have classes with master gurus and just 15 students. The reality is that if master gurus teach only classes with 15 students, that the vast majority of students will never ever be able to take a class from a particular master guru. The economics suggest that the majority of students would never ever be able to afford to take a class from a master guru.

So master gurus, subject-matter experts, will be better put to use teaching large classes of 100 or more students in them, especially when the master guru's area of expertise really is in the subject matter rather than andragogy, discussion facilitation, needs assessment, or grading.

Other benefits for all

Light rail and trains will also have many other benefits for everyone in society. Trains will enable our youth to be less overweight and healthier. Our children are couch potatoes because adults are car potatoes. People taking light rail and trains walk more, are less overweight and are healthier. There is no drinking while intoxicated (DWI or DUI) on trains, saving lives, societal cost, and regulatory effort. Trains pollute far less than cars. Light rail and trains are way much safer than cars. With around 80% of cars having only one person in them, there is more face-to-face communication on light rail and trains. With cars constituting a major expense and physical item, the family budget has more flexibility and is less burdened by material things. And without cars, there is little need for garages and other places devoted to car space.

In summary, transportation has always had a critical impact on education, whether it was the number of miles a child could walk to the one-room schoolhouse, or the school bus taking students to the factory school of today.

Trains will have a similar critical impact on education in the 21st century. Trains will allow students at the elementary and secondary level the choice to attend the best school for them in a typical 200-mile range. Trains will redesign higher education campuses, creating systems of campuses with more resources. And trains will impact the pedagogy of the 21st century, creating the logistical opportunity and framework within which teachers and students learn and teach differently, and better.

Chapter 9.
Finances: Building 21st Century Schools and Colleges

There are two financial challenges and imperatives to financing the schools and colleges of the 21st century.

The first challenge and imperative is for education to have increased financial support from taxpayers and society. As we moved from the one-room schoolhouse of the 19th century into the Industrial Age school of the 20th century, taxpayer support for education greatly increased. It was made possible, of course, by a substantial increase in the standard of living for most people. It is unlikely that we can provide the education necessary for preparing a person to be a knowledge worker, including a four-year college degree, at the same or less money we spent to prepare people to be factory workers or farmers.

The second challenge and imperative that has to be undertaken concurrently with the request for more public support is the need to restructure and redesign the financing of our schools and colleges for the 21st century. Without a financial restructuring, any increase in financial support will be both ineffective educationally and a wasteful expenditure monetarily.

For K-12 education, the financial objective is to prepare twice as many of its students to enter and graduate from college.

For higher education, the financial objective is to double enrollments, double graduation rates, and do it for less than double the cost.[1]

Clearly, the financial model for higher education is broken. Only 55% of youth who enter college or university graduate. This is approaching the wasting of half of money spent on higher education. This is like paying twice as much for each college graduate as we should. This is akin to the costly health care system in the United States that led to health care reform. Some university presidents have already recognized that the financial model is broken. It becomes more painfully obvious each year into the new century.

Here are some of the things that can be done to make elementary and secondary education more cost effective.
- Use school buildings 18 hours a day, holding classes for younger students earlier, for older students later, and for community, use both early and late in the day and evening.
- Move classes to being hybrid, saving space and increasing teacher engagement time with students.
- Move responsibility for gyms and pools to the community, sharing such facilities with adults in the community.
- Increase online learning at all levels.
- Engage software to do many of the administrative and record-keeping tasks currently done manually.
- Boost teacher engagement time with students by reducing their time spent in behavior management, administration, and meetings.

When elementary and secondary schools begin to prepare more students to be accepted in, and graduate from, college, then additional public support can be requested.

Here are some of the things that can be done to make higher education more cost effective.
- Eliminate capital funding budgets, eliminate new buildings, and refit existing buildings to have more classrooms.
- Make all classes hybrid, halving the requirement for classroom space.
- Get rid of administrative and faculty offices, refitting the space for classroom use.
- Hold classes 18 hours a day.
- Increase the percentage of time faculty is engaged in teaching from 55% to 75%.

There are two kinds of expenditures that are right:
- Those expenses that lead to learning and knowledge (computers, wireless access) which every student (as defined at 90% or above) should have.
- Other expenses directly related to learning and knowledge that are tailored to the individual, necessary or vital for a specific student, such accommodation for a dog for the autistic student, or art supplies for the art student.

The overarching objective is to ensure that at least half of our society's youth have a four-year college degree. And that doubling of output has to be done at less than double the cost; that is, it has to be done more efficiently and productively. In order for that 21st century mandate to be accomplished, the financial model for education has to be redesigned. There are at least four critical areas where budgeting changes have to be made.

1. Technology
Technology expenses have to increase dramatically. Almost all of the technology is related to the Internet. Students require computers and high-speed access to the Internet from anyplace in the school and college. Schools and colleges need more servers, server power, and software. All courses need online classrooms. The latest software needs to be purchased. Some institutions will even benefit by creating their own customized software.

All technology expenses are a good investment. But some technology expenses will even save money in the short run. Computers for students may reduce textbook costs. Online classrooms will save costs on up to half of all classroom space. Software exists that will save teachers and administrators considerable time, time that can be reallocated towards critical mission central activities. The rule in this century is that if technology can do a function, then technology must do that function. And software is being created that will allow students and teachers to accomplish things unheard of only a few years ago. There is, or will be:
- a program to analyze student learning strengths,
- a program to tell the teacher how to engage a particular student better,
- a program that automatically finds the best online resources to respond to an individual student's learning style; and much more.

The sum total of online software is both saving teacher and student time, but also enhancing student learning. Technology is essential to education today.

2. Buildings

Buildings and the associated physical plant aspects (lawns, parking lots, etc.) are a financial and unsustainable albatross on all educational institutions today.

In the last century buildings were the goal, the symbol of success, the enduring legacy of school officials. Buildings were something of which to be proud, having more was better, and leaving buildings to future generations was an achievement.

In this century, buildings are simply a cost. They are a burden. They have to be minimized, reduced, redesigned, or just simply eliminated. Every expense for something physical and tangible has to be questioned. And expenses that require future expenditures in maintenance, utilities, and personnel have to be avoided except in absolute necessary circumstances.

For example, in four-year higher education, institutions are spending way too much on buildings. Writes William A. Daigneau, Director for University Facilities at the University of Rochester, "Higher education is generally recognized as a highly labor-intensive industry. Often, salaries and related benefits costs represent 70 to 80 percent of an institution's annual operating expenses. However, few people understand that higher education is also highly capital intensive. Colleges and universities in the United States own or operate approximately 3 billion square feet of building space. With an estimated replacement value of more than $300 billion, higher education's investment in plant is the single largest asset on its balance sheet, eclipsing many times the value of the more liquid, and hence more visible, financial endowments. On average, each of the 3,300 colleges and universities in the United States owns or operates property valued at almost $100 million."[2]

New buildings are so valued that they have their own budget, called a capital budget, which is separate from the operating budget in institutions of higher education.

Yet William F. Lasher and Deborah L. Greene note, "New facilities burden the operating budget with additional expenditures for utilities and maintenance, while renovated facilities usually lessen the burden." [3]

3. Teachers

Financial resources devoted to teachers and faculty have to be bolstered and reinforced, albeit in responsible financially viable and societally acceptable ways. This in no way means that all or even most teacher and faculty salaries and benefits should be increased. It does mean that an educational institution's quality and success is totally dependent on the quality of its instructors.

Faculty members need more professional development, and it has to be better professional development. Teacher and faculty salaries have to be competitive and sufficient to recruit superior teachers. At the same time, faculty members need more accountability, revised job descriptions, and there needs to be a system for helping underperforming teachers to exit the field. But overall, if teacher performance is to meet expectations of students, parents, and society at large, financial resources have to be available to make that happen.

To illustrate this situation in higher education, Robert K. Toutkoushian reports that during the period 1974 to 1995, instructional costs declined by 5 percent of the average budget at a four-year university, down to 42% of the budget, while six other major categories in university budgets rose as a percentage of the overall budget.[4]

4. Non-Instructional Activities

Non-instructional activities, whether they are student activities, teacher activities, administrative activities, or the personnel associated with non-instructional activities, have to be reduced or eliminated.

The top administrators in educational institutions at all levels spend up to half of their time on non-instructional activities. Some administrative jobs are devoted entirely to non-instructional activities.

The laundry list of non-instructional activities that have to be questioned is long - lunch rooms, video monitors, mowing lawns, sports teams, clubs, school buses, dormitories, weight rooms, parades, homecoming dances, mascots, detention rooms, study hall monitors, custodians, parking lots, attendance taking, clothing policies, and more.

In elementary and secondary schools, there are activities that should be assumed by the community at large instead of the schools. In colleges and universities, there are activities that simply have no place there.

Financially, the cost of non-instructional activities keeps rising. There does not appear to be any ceiling, any ideal benchmark or standard, or any cost-benefit analysis that would make non-instructional activities justified given limited resources and the unmet imperative of learning and knowledge.

To illustrate this at the higher education level, Larry L. Leslie and Gary Rhoades write, "By essentially any measure, administrative costs in colleges and universities have risen dramatically during the past two decades, disproportionately more than the costs of instruction and research. Accelerating a four-decade pattern, expenditures for presidents, deans and their assistants grew 26 percent faster than instructional budgets in the 1980s."[5]

When educational institution budgets are analyzed, there is:
• way too little spent on technology,
• not enough spent on boosting faculty expertise and productivity,
• way too much spent on buildings and physical facilities, and
• unsustainable amounts spent on non-instructional activities and personnel.

It is not necessarily that we spend too little on education. An OECD analysis determined that in 2003 "the United States spent 2.9 percent of its GDP on postsecondary institutions. This was far higher than the OECD average of 1.4 percent and, indeed, higher than any other country for which data were reported."[6] But it is certainly the case that we spend our education resources on the wrong things.

Calling them 'failure factories,' Mark Schneider notes, "College graduation rates are worse than high school graduation rates. The costs of this abysmal performance to students and taxpayers are high."[7]

The result is that in the United States, too much money is spent on education at all levels - elementary, secondary and higher education - for the results achieved, and those results are only half of what education needs to achieve in order to create a prepared workforce and sufficient societal prosperity.

What schools and colleges will look like

The first thing to understand about this issue is that the physical space for schools and colleges will be a secondary issue. In the last century, schools and colleges started with the physical building, and then built curriculum, hired teachers, and created activities around this starting point of a physical building.

This was in keeping with the so-called "edifice complex" of the last century, where businesses celebrated their success and size with buildings. There was a Sears Tower in Chicago, a Chrysler Building in New York, and so on. In this century many of the leading companies emphasize their web sites, not their buildings. Somewhere, for example, Amazon and Google have buildings, but they are secondary to their web sites. Their businesses are built around their web sites, not their buildings.

In the same way, schools and colleges will be built around their web sites and their faculty, not around a physical space. The web sites will be a combination of public web sites, Intranets or private password protected areas, virtual offices and online classrooms.

In most schools and colleges today, if you walked into a classroom, you would see desks all lined up in rows, with a teacher area up front. This is the classic pyramid or organizational structure in physical form. Your only clue as to whether the classroom was in an elementary school, secondary school or college might be the size of the students' desks.

In the 21st century, only a minority of schools and colleges will be totally virtual, with little or no physical space. Most schools and colleges will have a physical space, one or more buildings, and physical classrooms, with these characteristics.

Physical design. The physical design of a classroom will almost certainly be in the shape and function of a network.

Function. The function of the physical classroom will almost certainly be to encourage, foster and conduct collaborative learning as much or more than individualized learning.

Customization. The space will be created to allow and sustain students learning and being taught in different ways, unlike the one-size-fits-all model of the factory classroom.

Physical space for elementary and secondary schools

Some schools in the United Kingdom have adopted the model of a physical classroom with tables rather than individual desks. There are four students seated at each table, intentionally assigned seats so that an above-average student is seated kitty-corner to a below-average student, and two average students are seated kitty-corner to each other. The physical seating promotes student interaction that maximizes learning for all four students.

A high school in Australia has gained worldwide attention for pioneering another model, which they call a "learning commons." "At

Coburg Senior High school," writes student Jake Harman, "there are no old-style classrooms, no blackboards and no teachers at the front of the classroom. Instead there is a new style of classroom called learning commons which are open-planned areas where students interact and work effectively." (8) It is composed of a very large and open room, with plenty of windows, light and outside view. Within the room are many tables, the size and shape of which may vary. The room has high-speed Internet access. Students gather at a table, either scheduled or spontaneously, and have freedom of movement within the school. Teachers also go to the tables, either scheduled or spontaneously. And this is where the majority of student-student physical interaction and student-teacher physical interaction takes place.

Harman adds, "There are spaces which offer privacy or silence for students when needed, such as when voice recording. Students can use one of many conference rooms scattered around the school. These offer solitude and are used often for meetings and personal study sessions. These new classrooms offer a chance for students to learn in completely different and more effective ways," he concludes.

At the time of this writing, this open planned classroom, which the Australian school calls a learning commons, appears to be the leading candidate for the physical design of a classroom.

As communities become densely organized around light rail and train stations, schools will have their physical locations in these dense neighborhoods as well so students can either walk or take the train. Schools might have entire buildings, or they might have one or more individual rooms in various locations.

Physical space for colleges

At the time of this writing, colleges and universities have created few if any models for the physical classroom of the 21st century. While faculty and higher education institutions have made exciting history and success pioneering the asynchronous teacher-led online classroom, they have up until this point left the physical classroom unchanged from the factory model. That will certainly change.

It is highly unlikely that elementary and secondary students, raised in collaborative learning situations and classrooms, preparing to work in business organizations that will demand collaborative work, will go from collaborative learning spaces in secondary school back to the factory classroom upon entering college and university.

Instead, it is most likely that when a collaborative physical class-room model becomes more established, recognized, accepted and thus more universal, colleges and universities will retrofit existing class-rooms and build new ones with the physical classroom model intact. There will also be specialized rooms, such as music studios, art rooms, biology laboratories, and even a traditional lecture hall here and there. Like elementary and secondary schools, colleges and universities will be located near or at train or light rail stations. They may retain a campus, or simply be composed of buildings, or even scattered class-room locations. Like elementary and secondary schools, they will almost certainly consolidate and share resources with other colleges and universities, so that one campus or college might have a physics lab used by other colleges within the same system or cooperative or coalition.

In summary, what we know now is that the physical space for schools and colleges will be a consequence of the pedagogy adopted by schools and colleges for the 21st century, not a determinant of the pedagogy. Andragogy, pedagogy, web sites and teacher roles will all be primary in the shaping of the 21st century school or college. When there is some sort of consensus on the pedagogical foundation of education in the 21st century, then educational institutions will revise the physical space. Physical space will be modified and created to meet the learning needs, situations and conditions of students, not deter-mine them.

Section II.
Towards Personalization

We know some of the tools that will enable educators to personalise learning and teaching.

The Internet will be used extensively and pervasively, providing both students and teachers with tools to respond to different learning styles, access unlimited content, assess and measure learning using multiple assessments corresponding with individual testing needs, and much more.

The role of the teacher will change, with far less focus on delivering content and far more focus on helping students learn. Learner engagement time will increase, time diverted to worrying about behavior will be reduced, and specialized functions like testing and assessment will be contracted out to specialists, and physical space and time of day will be redesigned to create a more efficient and effective learning environment.

We also know that all of this will not happen at once, and yet there are things each of us can do now to begin to personalise our teaching and to begin to help create the new model for education.

In this section we explore three of those places where we can start to personalise learning and teaching now.

The first aspect is understanding the neurology of learning and the brain, as new knowledge is created continually about how we learn and how we can help our students to learn by understanding more about how the brain and the body work to facilitate learning.

The second aspect is gender, as we know relatively a lot about how females and males learn differently. We can teach each sex differently to maximize the learning for both our male and our female students.

And thirdly, the issue of Asperger's and autism in many of our students illustrates why in this century no one is normal, and the factory model categorization of learners as "normal" (the ideal) and "special" is obsolete. It demonstrates why the label "disability" needs to be replaced by the concept and practice of determining strengths and weaknesses and differing learning styles, so the talents and skills of each student can be maximized. And it gives us another "to-do" place to start in our understanding and practice of tailoring and customizing the educational experience for each of our students. In this section we suggest there are ways we can get started now in personalising education.

Chapter 10.
The Neurology of Learning

What is the purpose of the brain? Julie remembers, "Sitting in my seventh grade math class, the teacher was telling one student that learning math was important, and concentrating on the material was essential. 'That,' he said, 'is why you have a brain.'" Many teachers probably believe that the function of the brain is to learn algebra or to learn how to diagram sentences, or to be able to read and interpret great literature. Indeed, our brains are capable of all these tasks, but that is not why we have a brain. We have a brain for only one purpose, and that purpose is survival. The function of the brain is to allow us, as living beings, to understand and respond to our environment in ways that will assure that we survive and propagate our species. This function is no different from that of any other creature in the universe.

Because our brain's top priority is keeping us alive, there are certain functions that have evolved over the thousands of years of our existence, and which are "hard-wired" in our neurological functioning. They are responses and reactions to the environment that occur when we find ourselves in certain types of situations. In previous ages, these responses were key to our survival. The fight-or-flight response, for example is a response to threat that results in a variety of physiological reactions that prepare us to meet and defeat a threat. While this response was very helpful when someone was being chased by a predator or an enemy, it is less useful in responding to many of the kinds of threats that humans encounter in today's modern, technological world.

The fight-flight response is one of many reactions that are hard-wired and which occur without our conscious action. For teachers, it is critical to understand how the brain works in order to be successful in helping students learn at their optimal level. In his book, *Decartes' Error*[1], Antonio Demasio offers an intriguing view of the relationship between mind and body, and challenges the artificial distinction between the two. His is a revolutionary analysis of how emotion and reason interact within the mind to create our actions, beliefs and decisions. Emotion and reason are not separate from each other in his portrait of the mind. They are both inextricable parts of how we function as human beings. The interaction of emotion and reason are critical to understand in our classrooms, and the autonomic functions of the brain essential to take into account in the teaching/learning relationship.

This chapter is necessarily limited to highlighting some of the key neurological functions that are at play when students learn, and we will focus on those that have some of the highest impact on student success. We have looked at some ways in which the human brains respond differently, based on gender. Now we will take a look at some of the ways that human brains respond more generally. This information can inform classroom practice in ways that will contribute substantially to student success.

Some Facts about the Brain

In their book, *Making Connections: Teaching and the Human Brain,*[2] Caine and Caine put forth twelve principles of how the brain functions in learning:

1. *"The brain is a complex and adaptive system."* It functions at many levels at one time, and "Thoughts, emotions, imagination, predispositions and physiology operate concurrently and interactively as the entire system interacts with and exchanges information with its environment." It is essential that educators understand this complex aspect of how the brain affects human learning.

2. *"The Brain is a social brain."* Our interactions with others and social systems contribute mightily to who we are. Our brains change throughout life in response to the social systems in which we operate. Finding our identity and a sense of belonging are critical to learning. For teachers this means being inclusive and making every student feel valued and accepted.

3. *"The search for meaning is innate."* This means that as a survival strategy, we seek to make meaning of our experiences. It is a basic drive that lasts a lifetime, and that changes over time as we make sense of our experiences in different ways.

4. *"The search for meaning occurs through patterning."* Our brains automatically register what is familiar and seek out what is new. That is why we may not be able to accurately describe in detail things we see or experience regularly. They are familiar to us, and we "know" what they are about. As learners sort through information that is both familiar and new, they construct patterns of understanding that are meaningful to them. This is a critical aspect of education.

5. *"Emotions are critical to patterning."* As Demasio points out[3], emotions and thoughts are linked and cannot be separated. Emotions influence meaning and in turn affect expectations, perceptions, self-esteem, social comfort and learning. An experience may create an emotional response that lasts a lifetime, and therefore, a proper emotional climate is essential to educating learners well. Here is an example. A few years ago, the authors interviewed Langdon Divers, a man who was then 102 years old. The purpose was to learn more about what life was like a century ago. During the interview, Mr. Divers shared some of his experiences in school. He talked about a time when he was frequently late for class because he became preoccupied in watching the ships unloading in harbor every morning. His teacher was very displeased about this, and considered it disrespectful and unacceptable. At the end of the term, students were given a final exam and also asked to turn in their lab notes. Mr. Divers did not have his notes. Even though he was the only student to receive an "A" on the exam, his teacher gave him an "F" because he did not turn in his notes and because he was frequently tardy. In those days, the "F" meant repeating an entire year of school, which he was forced to do before going on to University study and becoming an engineer. After telling this story, Mr. Divers looked at me beseechingly and asked, with a catch in his voice, "He didn't handle that right, did he?" After more than 85 years, this event from the past still affected him and triggered strong negative emotions. That teacher's actions had never been put to rest for him.

6. *"Every brain simultaneously perceives and creates parts and wholes."* This means that we use both sides of our brain in everything we do. We see the whole and relate parts to the global picture. That is why teachers need to provide the big picture as well as the parts in every learning activity.

7. *"Learning involves both focused attention and peripheral perception."* Learners take in information of which they are consciously aware, but also information that is not part of their direct attention. This, too, is an innate survival strategy. In prehistoric times, being aware of things outside the immediate focus was essential to help individuals understand environmental changes that might represent danger. In today's world, these outside signals are still very powerful. Teachers can unconsciously send signals that may show their personal feelings, beliefs, and attitudes, and this can profoundly affect learner. Thus, attending to the minute details of the learning environment is a critical element in good teaching.

8. *"Learning always involves conscious and unconscious processes."* Understanding is a complex process. While some learning takes place in the classroom and is based on information of which the student is directly aware, much learning also takes place outside the classroom hours, days, or even weeks after information is presented. Processing the information, creating the patterns that enhance understanding and learning are unconscious processes that occur over time. For teachers, providing activities that enhance the learner's ability to create meaning from information and experiences is an important aspect of what they do.

9. *"We have at least two ways of organizing memory."* Caine and Caine draw on the work of O'Keefe and Nadel to explain the two basic ways that we process memory. One way is used to recall relatively unrelated experiences and is based on reward and punishment —conditioned responses. The other is always active and is based on novelty. Thus, they suggest, we have the biological capacity to store both meaningful and seemingly meaningless experiences, and it is the integration of these experiences, stored separately in the brain, that results in learning.

10. *"Learning is developmental."* Neurologists have written much about the plasticity of the brain. This means that our brains are adaptive. They change over time in response to the stimuli and experiences we encounter. This plasticity influences the hard-wiring of our brains, and the sequential steps which humans experience in their development provides the tools and structures for later learning. Neurologists have now determined that our brains continue to create new connections throughout life, and that learning literally "has no end."

11. *"Complex learning is enhanced by challenge and inhibited by threat."* We learn best when our brains are alert and challenged, but when threatened, our brains revert to more primitive functioning and become less flexible and less responsive. There can be a fine line between challenge and threat. One university professor confided in me that he was baffled about why so many of his students "gave up" and dropped his course so easily. One of the things he tried to do, he said, was to give them tough quizzes to help them identify where they needed to focus their learning. Instead of challenging them, this practice seemed to defeat them. He, himself noted that when he was in school, this sort of activity was motivating. Students today, he concluded, are just not motivated like the used to be. This example illustrates many of the principles we have considered so far. The experiences of today's students are different from the experiences of those 40 years ago, and their classroom responses may not be expected to be the same. This is not related to their lack of motivation, but to the complex interaction of emotions and reason that impact their learning behavior.

12. *"Every brain is uniquely organized."* Every snowflake is unique. Each has a crystalline structure, each is formed by a formation of water molecules and thus each has the same make-up as far as systems and content. However, many factors affect the formation of a snowflake; variations in temperature, the height of the clouds in which they formed, environmental pollution, humidity, and other factors affect the formation of a snowflake. It is still true, that we all recognize snowflakes when we see them, even though they are all different. The same is true of our brains. All our brains have the same systems

and basic structure, but many factors influence how our brains develop. Environment, genetics, and our individual experiences are some factors that influence how our brains develop. Because no two individuals have identical environment, genetics and experiences, there are no two identical brains. The result is the huge diversity of talent, skills, intelligences, and learning styles that we encounter among learners. Understanding and respecting the uniqueness of the human brain is another key aspect of being an excellent teacher.

Seven Points of Intervention

Jeb Schenck, PhD, is both a high school teacher and college instructor. Speaking on building boys' success,[4] Schenck presents workshops on how to incorporate brain-based teaching into the classroom. The following strategies demonstrate concrete strategies that can be used which respond to the principles outlined by Caine and Caine. In his presentation he discussed seven points of intervention in the classroom that can improve learning and which respond to basic principles of how our brains function.

1. Attention

The first point of intervention is attention. It is important, before beginning any lesson, to make sure you have the students' attention. This can be accomplished in many ways, and may include short exercises that are fun, humorous and which have no relationship to the lesson itself. This kind of exercise helps to make the brain more alert and attentive and prepares it for learning. In the workshop Schenck used the following exercise:

When participants entered the room, there was a twenty-dollar bill prominently taped to the podium. It was impossible not to see it. Of course it got attention, and everyone wondered what it was for. Before beginning his presentation, Schenck told participants that he wanted to have a short exercise. He asked each participant to write a definition of intelligence. Whoever got the answer right would earn the twenty dollars. Of course, this focused attention and got the participants to think about intelligence.

When all answers were read, he informed the group that all were wrong. In fact, there is no agreed-upon definition of intelligence, so he kept the twenty dollars, but the participants were engaged and ready to learn.

2. Emotion

Emotion can enhance or inhibit learning.
- Emotions affect attention.
- Emotions affect motivation.
- Emotions affect working memory.
- Emotions affect long term memory.
- Emotions affect review.
- Emotions affect assessment.

3. Motivation

Motivation is linked to emotion. Students are often in "survival mode" in your classroom. When students enter the classroom, they are filled with all kinds of emotions which can interfere with learning. Maybe they are upset with their teacher from the last class, maybe they just took a test they fear they failed, maybe there are issues outside of school that are distracting them. Whatever the source, Schenck says that it is important to deal with this aspect of students' reality and offer a chance to set some of these feelings aside. If they feel a threat, there is a threat. Lowering that threat level is key to learning. To do this, he said that he often begins his class with a short free-discussion period where students are free to discuss anything they want to with the class or with other students. Even if they do not discuss the specific fear or conflict that is of immediate concern, this gives students a chance to find a bit of equilibrium before diving into the lesson.

You can have a big influence on your students' motivation in other ways as well through:
- Your demeanor
- Your passion for what you do
- How they perceive that you relate to them.

You should also strive to create a healthy classroom:
- Provide a physical and social environment
  conducive to learning.
- Involve students in goal-setting.
- Encourage self-assessment.
- Allow mistakes without penalty.

You can also demonstrate to students that they are capable of performing the task. Let them see someone else at their level do it successfully. This is a powerful motivator. Help them answer the questions:

- Can I do it?
- Have I seen someone else (a peer) do it?
- Why should I want to do it?
- What do I need to succeed?

Students learn best when they believe they can do the task, when they believe there is a good reason to learn how to do the task, and when they believe they have what it takes to succeed.

Motivate your students by meeting the three basic needs they have for:

- Belonging
- Having choices
- Feeling competent.

Make your classroom a safe environment and demonstrate your respect for each student. When students feel they belong, they are more successful. There are many ways to provide choices or options - for example, students may choose to answer one of three questions on an exam or to do a project or a report. They may be given the opportunity to decide about what materials or resources to use. These choices can lead to a greater sense of competence on the part of students, and contribute to their success.

4. Working memory

There are two kinds of memory - working memory and long-term memory. Working memory is short-term memory. Students can hold information in their working memory for about 60 to 90 seconds before it is either pushed into long-term memory or lost. Not only is short-term memory temporary, but it is also limited. The brain can hold only a limited amount of information in short-term memory before it becomes overloaded. There are several ways to enhance the effectiveness of short-term memory.

Pause and allow time for processing. The brain needs processing time. This means that there needs to be time when the brain is "free" to sort, categorize and store information that has been taken in. We all understand that the brain has circadian rhythms that we experience during sleep. We are less aware that these rhythms are at play during our waking hours. These brain rhythms follow approximate ninety-minute cycles. Thus, the block schedules in many high schools today provide an optimal time period for instruction. About every 90 minutes, the brain will take a short "break" where attention lapses. Changing classes and other activities that may occur as part of the students' routines do not count as "processing time." Students need actual shifts in activities that free them to process and store new information.

Further, according to Eric Jensen, author of *Teaching with the Brain in Mind*, "genuine, external attention can be sustained at a high a constant level for only a short time, generally about 10 minutes or less"[5]. Thus, good teachers will pause in their instruction or introduce other activities such as group discussion to allow students to process information they have just been given. Talk and discussion is one critical aspect of learning and retention. Additionally, it is very helpful if teachers provide access to key information through handouts and online resources. Taking notes may interfere with attention and retention. At the 2010 Annual Conference on Distance Teaching and Learning held at the University of Wisconsin in Madison, two teachers discussed their strategies for using technology to enhance student success. One of their strategies was to post all notes and handouts online for all students, leaving them free to attend more directly to the classroom instruction[6].

Present information in chunks. By organizing information systematically so that it relates logically to other information you provide, learning is enhanced. That is the reason that phone numbers are written as a series of numbers separated by dashes, rather than one long number. It is easier to remember the information when it is presented in chunks.

5. Long-Term Memory

A key goal of teaching is to help students move their experiences into their long-term memory. There are several strategies, based on brain theory that can help with this.

- Overload. Be aware that learners who are tired and sleep-deprived are not as efficient in learning as those who are well-rested. Scheduling the most cognitively demanding courses during the times of day when students are likely to have the most energy is a sound strategy. Also, schools that have moved to schedules that begin later in the morning have found that performance among high school students improves.
- Link information to other activities. This is called "procedural

memory" and the act of physical movement, when linked to an idea or concept can trigger the recollection of that concept. This is a very effective way of helping students retain information in long-term memory.
• Write it down. Asking students to write down key information is another way to enhance memory. This does not mean writing it down by taking notes but by providing assignments where they are able to write out the key concepts, facts and information that they need to remember.
• Talk about it. Talking, explaining a concept to other students or discussing it also improves recall. Often, peer teaching and discussion are the most effective ways to help students move information into long-term memory.

6. Practice past perfection

This is a strategy where students review and repeat information that they have learned - not to the point of boredom, but to the point where they will be able to recall it easily. Practicing past perfection leads to mastery.

7. Assessment

The final point of intervention that leads to increased student success is assessment. There are some strategies for assessment that can help students perform competently and demonstrate what they have learned.
• First, your assessment should match what you present and practice in your classroom. It is counterproductive to assess based on what students may "infer" from your presentation or what they have practiced. That does not reflect what they have learned. You need to assess understanding, not the ability of students to transfer what they have learned to unfamiliar situations.
• Match the sophistication of your review to the level of your assessment. Any effective review must give students information about the level of information they will need to know for any test or exam, project or paper. If the review covers concepts but at a simpler level than the assessment, it will not help students study or prepare properly.
• Your assessment should be in the same style and level as your teaching. What your students have learned is based on how and what you have presented. Proper assessment will allow them to

demonstrate that.

- Use multiple assessment tools. It is undeniable that some students are more capable in using different communication modes. Verbal, written, and hands-on options for demonstration of learning are assessment choices that you can make available so that you can see what your students have actually learned, not just how they are best at communicating.

In summary, understanding the principles of brain function and how they impact learning among students of all ages is an area where there has, up to now, been inadequate information and training for teachers. As we have been able, through new technologies, to understand in greater depth how our brains work and how that affects learning, it is essential that every teacher understand and practice teaching based on how the brain functions.

Chapter 11.
Inside the Male and Female Brain

In 1920, M. V. O'Shea, Professor of Education at the University of Wisconsin in Madison, published one of a series of books on education and parenting. Referring to adolescence as "the crucial age," he describes the rapid physical changes that occur at puberty, and of youth he writes, "The brain could not, of course, remain dormant while all the other organs [are] undergoing metamorphosis. It is the last to receive adolescent stimulus, but the change is most profound when it does come. Cerebral areas that have lain dormant up until this time now make ready for functioning. . . ." He also notes of brain development that "When an organ is expanding with extraordinary rapidity, it cannot expend as relatively large an amount of energy in action as under normal conditions. . . .When it is largely drawn upon at one point, the amount that can be employed at other points must be decreased.[1]

While the language is quaint and the conclusions based upon observation and anecdote, the modern field of neuroscience has, through the use of sophisticated technology and empirical methodologies, come to much the same conclusions as Dr. O'Shea, and has gone even farther in examining how biology impacts behavior both inside and outside of the educational setting. Through the use of neuro-imaging and brain scans, we are now able to know more than we have ever known about the brain and how it works. Even more illuminating is the fact that we can literally see the differences in how the male brain and the female brain function.

The biological differences in the brain account for many of the

129

gender-based differences in behavior we see in the classroom and in the workplace. Much of what has, in the past, been attributed to cultural or societal bias is in fact strongly influenced by biological differences. Our complex system of societal relationships did, undeniably, lead to the institutionalization of systematic, discriminatory, gender-biased practices in education in the past. For example, Dr. O'Shea writes, "In the matter of education, too, we have given the boy much more freedom than we have allowed the girl. We have said to the former: 'Go as far as you like in the pursuit of knowledge. . . .Go deeply into science or history or economics or mathematics, or literature or whatever attracts you. The more deeply you go, the more highly we will regard you.' But we have said to the girl: 'It will be better for you to study light subjects, as art and language and literature. It is not quite the thing for a girl to try to master such subjects as biology or chemistry or engineering or agriculture and so on.'"

Even so, Dr. O'Shea notes in 1920, women were beginning to "break the artificial restrictions" and were entering the fields of math, science, and "even engineering" in increasing numbers. "The history of modern education tells an illuminating story of woman's ascendency in educational activities and achievement. Even after women were admitted to colleges on a par with men, they were not considered to be capable of attaining a high degree of scholarship. In a brief period, though, they have climbed to the highest point reached by men, and now they are crowding ahead of them." Indeed, the academic achievements of women were threatening to many conservative collegians - so threatening that the governors of the Phi Beta Kappa society proposed that the number of women admitted should be arbitrarily limited. Their rationale was that "unless a check is thus put upon women, they will soon outnumber the men and the society will become a feminine organization."

This basic argument which was erupting one hundred years ago is essential to understanding some of the issues that face educators today. Gender issues have not disappeared, but they are profoundly different from those of the early part of the twentieth century. The pendulum has swung so far in the direction of supporting girls and women that it can be quite risky to suggest that there may be differences in how males and females learn or that, even worse, there may be things that boys can do better than girls. No such risk exists in asserting that there are things that girls might do better than boys, however. To a great extent, the remarkable achievements of women in the past three decades are the result of a conscious effort to eliminate discriminatory practices that might pose barriers for women. The awareness that the first half of the century did, indeed, place intentional roadblocks in the path of women was a key to righting the system. If we are to successfully address some of the fundamental flaws in our educational processes, we must be able to go beyond the knee-jerk reaction that every institution in our society remains biased against women. In the early 20th century there was a profound shift in gender roles in the United States. Women got the vote. Women were accepted into colleges and universities; they could drive cars, smoke cigarettes in public, and drink beer. They could bob their hair and show their ankles. They could be decision makers and leaders in the business world. The world was turned upside-down, and these changes were very threatening to the traditionalists. Change is always hard to accept, and discrimination was real and oppressive for women.

By the middle of the twentieth century, women had made great strides toward equality in education and work. By the end of the twentieth century there was no difference in what women could choose as a career and what men could choose. Women were now doctors, attorneys, pilots, Secretarys of State, Presidential contenders, Vice Presidential candidates, senators, governors, engineers, corporate CEOs, professional athletes, and combat soldiers. Women scientists outnumber men scientists, female physicians outnumber males, there are more women with Bachelor's degrees and Master's degrees than there are men, and there are equal numbers of men and women with Doctoral degrees. Overall, women have surpassed men in terms of completing secondary and post-secondary education with the gender gap almost completely reversed. In 2006, 10.3% of males and 8.3% of females dropped out of high school. In 2005/2006, women earned 62% of Associate's degrees, 58% of Bachelor's degrees, 60.0% of Master's degrees, and 48.9% of Doctorates. In 2016/2017, women are projected to earn 64.2% of Associate's degrees, 59.9% of Bachelor's degrees, 62.9% of Master's degrees, and 55.5% of Doctorates.[2] Yet society persists in the notion that all women are disadvantaged both in school and in the workplace.

As a society it is essential that we take a long and objective look at our notions of gender bias and how this impacts the way we educate our children. We need to open our minds to the idea that education is not a gender competition; it is a necessity for our survival. We may need to consider some new ideas: boys and girls learn differently, and we will have to teach them differently so that both girls and boys are successful in school. As we dissect the tangled threads of belief that have dominated society for the past century, a more realistic image of gender and education will emerge, and with it, a more viable approach to education.

Biology vs Culture

In his 1977 book, *The Dragons of Eden,* Carl Sagan was one of the first writers to describe the evolution of the brain in language that made the concepts accessible to non-scientists. The brain, from the most primitive structures (the limbic system) to the most advanced (the neo-cortex) is comprised of many areas of specialty of function that govern how the individual processes and understands information. *The Dragons of Eden,* which won the Pulitzer Prize, was a revelation for most readers. The idea that some of our behaviors are still guided by primitive structures deep in our brains was a revolutionary idea.[3]

As exciting and informative as Sagan's work was, current neuroscience research allows us to have an even deeper understanding of the human brain. Sagan, like the majority of us, drew no great distinction between the male brain and the female brain. Only in the last decade have we come to realize that there are profound differences in the structure of the male and female brains, and that stimuli and information are processed differently and even in different areas of the brain, based on gender. The brain, as Sagan so rightly asserted, evolved over thousands of years. Its primary function was to allow humans to adapt to the environments they inhabited - to survive - to propagate the species. This evolution of the brain meant that, depending upon gender roles in assuring that survival, the male and female brains evolved somewhat differently. Each gender had areas of specialty in assuring the security of the family. Those evolutionary differences are still there today, just as the most primitive functions of the human brain that reside in the limbic system are still there, and they are still influencing our behaviors and perceptions. In modern society, many of the needs that those differences evolved to meet are no longer there, but the brain has not changed as rapidly as our culture.

The Impact of Neurological Differences

The human brain becomes masculinized or feminized before birth as a result of being exposed to being exposed to testosterone and estrogen among other hormones. If the brain receives more testosterone in utero, it develops into a male brain, and more estrogen will result in a female brain. The hormones are produced by the mother, based on the chromosomal structure of the developing fetus. There is no brain that is wholly masculine or feminine, but there is a huge spectrum of difference between the male and female brains. This does not mean, of course that all women behave exactly alike or that all men behave identically. There is a broad spectrum of possible behaviors within the male and female brains. For example, most men are uncomfortable talking about their feelings, but many can do so quite easily. (4) What is most important to understand is that there are measurable, quantifiable differences in how most men and women respond to the same stimuli, and this is biologically based, not culturally determined. (5)

Here are some examples:

In this diagram, there is a line at an angle and below it is a set of 15 lines. The task is to look at the figure and in 10 seconds identify the line in the set that is at the same angle as the line at the top of the diagram. The test consists of twenty diagrams. Men score higher on this test than women, and it is theorized that this is because the male brain is wired for spatial tasks. In past studies, 65% of women have scored between 0 and 13 correct answers while 60 percent of men scored 18 to 20 correct answers. One theory suggests that exposure to higher levels of testosterone before birth gives men an added advantage because the hormone may stimulate the development of the right hemisphere of the brain. This is the side that contributes most to spatial awareness.

Women, on the other hand, outperformed men on tests of spatial memory. Respondents were given 60 seconds to memorize the location of objects in a box. Then, some objects were moved and respondents were asked to identify which ones. Points were earned for correct answers and deducted for wrong answers. Women performed better on this test than men, with women averaging 46% correct answers and men only 39%. Some scientists believe that women score higher on spatial memory tests because the corpus callosum, the part of the brain that links the right and left hemispheres, is a fifth larger in women. This means women can process visual and other signals at the same time more easily than men. There is also a theory that estrogen levels in women give them an added advantage in spatial memory.[6]

Dr. Simon Baron-Cohen, in his study of autism, conducted a large number of experiments to study brain function. The two tests we have just reviewed were part of his study. In spite of measurable differences in performances on a range of neurological tests, scientists agree that there are no gender-based differences in intelligence between men and women - only gender-based differences in specific areas of function. Women scored higher on tests measuring empathy. Men scored higher on tests measuring systemizing. These differences in how the brain is wired most likely play a major role in how students approach learning, and thus, it is important to take these differences into consideration in the classroom. Also, it is important to remember that men and women don't always fit neatly into their respective groups. A University of Cambridge study found that 17% of men have a 'female' empathizing brain and 17% of women have a 'male' systemizing brain.

Further, Baron-Cohen in his book, *The Essential Difference: Men, Women and the Extreme Male Brain,* notes that there are other measurable differences. Men have 4% more brain cells than women, and about 100 grams more of brain tissue. Men have more gray matter, but women have more white matter. Women also have more dendritic connections between brain cells. A woman's brain has a larger corpus collusum, which means women can transfer data between the right and left hemisphere faster than men. Men tend to process more in the left brain while women have greater access to both sides. Women tend to use both sides of the brain to process language while men tend to process more often in the dominant hemisphere - typically the left side. This gives women a distinct advantage in language. Women have a larger deep limbic system than men. This gives them the ability to be more in touch with their feelings and to express them than men.[7]

It is also the case that the brain matures in a different sequence in males and females. Verbal skills mature much earlier in girls, as does the ability to understand non-verbal communication. For boys, maturity in abstract and spacial reasoning occurs earlier than in girls. Thus, in our contemporary educational system, we are requiring both male and female students to excel in areas where they are not developmentally ready to do so.

A Closer Look at the Male Brain

At one end of the spectrum is the most masculine brain possible. Such a brain would be low in serotonin, a neurotransmitter that plays an important role in memory, emotion, sleep and wakefulness; low oxyctocin, a hormone that is important to emotional behavior; a small corpus callosum and a small language center. The amygdala would be enlarged and have few neural pathways to the frontal lobes, and a small hippocampus with low-range pathways to emotive centers. In such a brain, there is not a lot of cross-communication between hemispheres. There are fewer aural neurons, so loud noises are not a problem. Consider the typical swashbuckling hero portrayed by John Wayne, a man of few words and much action, characterized by lack of emotion, aggressiveness and even impulsiveness. "He is very spatial and mechanical - he relies on objects moving in space with mechanical design - cars. . .guns, bullets, his own fists - enjoying more right hemisphere cortical use and less left".[8] Such a stereotype illustrates the extreme end of the spectrum of the masculine brain. While few individuals are as overwhelmingly imbued with the extreme characteristics portrayed here, the behavior of most males represents a less extreme version of the action hero. The male brain triggers behaviors and responses based on its structure and neurochemistry.

Some practical implications of gender differences

In understanding the structure and chemistry of the brain, we have the tools necessary to better understand some of the behaviors we observe in the classroom. Here are some differences in the male brain that neuroscientists have discovered and that can have a tremendous impact on learning, from *Boys and Girls Learn Differently* by Michael

135

Gurian and Patricia Henley.[9]

"Female brains excel at memory and sensory intake, while boys do better at spatial tasks and abstract reasoning. Boys tend to move emotive material 'down' in the brain to the more primitive brain stem, while girls move it up to the most advanced upper regions of the brain. This means that boys, whose brains are more task-focused and who actually are more fragile than girls, are more likely to become aggressive or withdraw and are more subject to being overwhelmed by stimuli. They cannot as easily overcome problems and move on to learn effectively. By contrast, girls can respond more flexibly to stimuli and are more prone to processing pain and seeking help from others." Competition motivates boys but too much stress will result in the "fight or flight" response (stand and defend).

Girls respond with "tend and amend." They turn to each other and build social networks to defend themselves.

Non-verbal communication is sometimes too subtle for boys. Many studies have found that girls fare better than boys in decoding non-verbal cues. (Hall, 1978). Although the percentages vary, communication studies suggest that much of what we communicate is based on non-verbal cues. Multiple studies have found that a large part percentage of communication is non-verbal. As much as 93% of communication may be delivered by non-verbal cues such as facial expression and inflection (Mehrabian, 1971). Although percentages vary, it is possible that male students may be at a disadvantage when communication is verbal.

A study by the Institute of Child Health in London found that at school entry, boys were 70% below the mean for girls in recognizing some non-verbal cues. Although these differences diminish over time, women remain more skilled in recognizing facial expressions and other non-verbal communications.

- Boys need to move around. Fidgeting, wiggling, and foot-tapping actually help boys focus.
- A resting female brain is as active as an activated male brain and thus has a learning advantage.
- Six times as many girls as boys can sing in tune. Girls hear better from birth, especially in the ranges of the female voice. Women not only hear better, but the ear responds more quickly. [10]
- Boys are less bothered by noise.
- Boys hear loud and low sounds better than high-pitched or soft sounds.[11]

- Not hearing can lead to loss of attention.
- Boys are not strong auditory learners.
- Males and females see differently, with boys doing better in brighter light and girls excelling in dim light.
- Males and females even taste differently, with females more sensitive to the bitter and preferring sweet tastes while males prefer salty foods.
- Hormonal differences between male and female were not as sharp a million years ago as they are today, since population growth results in more testosterone in men to prepare them for increased competition.
- Testosterone production varies throughout the year, and it is lowest in the spring. Some educators have speculated that this may in part account for lower ACT and SAT scores reported for males who take their tests in the spring.[12]
- The male and female brains mature in different sequences and at different rates:
- Boys are three times more likely to build a bridge out of blocks at age 3.
- Areas related to targeting and spatial memory mature 4 years earlier in boys than in girls.
- 3-year old girls could interpret facial expression as well as or better than 5 year old boys.
- Language and fine motor skills mature 6 years earlier in girls than in boys.[13]
- Girls are much quicker on timed tests than boys. Although a recent study of 8,000 people carried out at Vanderbilt University found that females handle timed tasks more quickly than boys, it found no overall intelligence difference by gender. The difference becomes pronounced in elementary school and is most pronounced among pre-teens and teenagers. This biological difference can put boys at a significant disadvantage in many academic situations.[14]

The Fundamental Difference

Overall, males and females are equal in intelligence. And they share most intellectual functions in common and to the same level. Young men and young women also test overall at roughly the same level.

But there are two significant differences in cognitive skills that greatly impact the learning of both female and male students.

There is so much scientific evidence, based on neurology and hormonal differences in the brain, that it is both impossible and counterproductive to ignore or rationalize these two differences.

Females are superior to males in terms of language skills.

This includes both verbal and written language skills. It does not mean every female is superior to every male; but overall, most females have superior language skills than most males.

The research suggests that females process language information using both sides of their brain, while males use only one side of the brain. They also process information in different areas of the brain. At the same time, females also have better neural connections between the areas of the brain devoted to emotion and to language, thus making it easier for females to express emotion.

Males are superior to females in terms of spatial skills.

It does not mean every male is superior to every female; but overall, most males have superior spatial skills than most females. Doreen Kimura, in her book *Sex and Cognition,* cites the evidence that spatial skill is linked to testosterone. She notes that studies have found that males receive three surges in testosterone levels. One surge is before birth, one in infancy, and one in the teen years. After each surge tests show males spatial skills increase over that of females' spatial skills at the same time.

Standardized tests administered by varying testing agencies over decades show this difference in cognitive skills between females and males on a consistent basis.

The scientific evidence about these two significant differences is so compelling, and the implications for enhancing both the learning of your male students and your female students so clear, that we call these two ying-yang variations "The Fundamental Difference" in how and why your male students learn differently than your female students.

As we have just stated, overall, males and females - - men and women, young men and young women, boys and girls - - are equally intelligent. There is no credible study that shows otherwise. Researchers on gender and intelligence make a point that the two sexes are equal in intelligence.

Equally important, young men and young women also test overall at roughly the same level. In their classic work, *Gender and Fair Assessment,* Educational Testing Service researchers Nancy S. Cole and Warren Willingham state, "Based on a wide variety of tests and a number of large nationally representative samples of high school seniors, we see no evidence of any consequential difference in the average test performance of young women and men."

For every educator, it is essential to understand that learning happens differently for males and females. Only when this happens, can we as educators assist both our female and male students to learn more and be able to perform optimally in school. In subsequent chapters we will examine specific ways in which teachers can respond to the learning needs of both male and female students in order to support their unique learning needs. The task will require setting aside some of our cultural myths, educating the educators about the neurology of learning, and developing specific strategies to create a more comfortable environment for learning.

In understanding gender and learning, there are a couple of additional important concepts related to the fundamental difference between female and male cognitive skills.

Gender

Gender characteristics are tendencies associated with one sex or the other. Scientists say that sex is almost always either/or. One is either male or female. Gender, however, is not either/or, as noted by Dr. Leonard Sax in *Why Gender Matters.* Gender characteristics are tendencies. When we speak of male characteristics or female characteristics, we are talking about tendencies. Not every female student will behave with entirely female characteristics, and not every male student will behave with entirely male characteristics. Nevertheless, most males will exhibit male characteristics, while most females will exhibit female characteristics.

Variability

Variability is the range of possible values for any measurable characteristic, physical or mental, of human beings. For every gender characteristic you will read in this book, you undoubtedly have or will encounter someone of the opposite sex with the same characteristic. In addition, people will have the gender characteristic in different amounts or proportion.

Twenty percent cross-over

The twenty percent cross-over concept is the finding that about 20% of one sex will have the characteristic or activity generally associated predominantly of the other sex. There is nothing abnormal in this. It is fascinating that in looking at the statistics for an activity predominantly associated with one sex or the other, the percent of the other sex participating is so often close to 20%.

Bell curve

The bell curve is a useful way of visualizing gender and variability. In most of the literature on gender and learning, the authors use one or more bell curves to visualize the distribution. Sometimes the bell curves for males and females are the same, and in some cases the bell curves for males and females differ compared to each other.

There is now a plethora of scientific evidence on the differences in neurology, hormonal influences, and brain structure and how these differences contribute to gender-based behavior in general and learning in particular. As educators, it is imperative that we understand the gender-based differences that account for much of student behavior in school, and address them in how we teach. It is essential to understand that learning happens differently for males and females.

Chapter 12.
Helping Male Students Succeed

In personalising our teaching, gender is one clear place to start. We know enough about how females and males learn differently to be able to begin teaching them differently. We know that teaching the two genders the same does a disservice to both males and females. And we now know the major educational challenges for students of each sex.

With our male students, there are two major educational challenges. The first, and most immediate challenge, is to help our male students to greater success in school and college. Males get worse grade point averages (GPA) than females, but more importantly, are a minority of college graduates. Yet overall, male students learn just as much as female students as evidenced by their overall test results, exhibit just as much responsibility in the workplace as females, and are just as intelligent as females. The second challenge involves teaching males differently than we teach our female students, understanding and then responding to the gender-based characteristics of males as learners.

One of the great achievements in education in the last half of the last century was to give women equal opportunity to attend and graduate from college. In 1960, only 40% of college graduates were female. By 1980 half of all graduates were women. Society will not retreat on its educational commitment to females. But for more than 30 years, since 1980, males have not graduated from college in equal numbers as females. Gender equity now means looking at gender bias from a different perspective, and how schools and teachers can treat male students equally.

College graduation: the immediate challenge

There are four interrelated issues with male students in higher education today:

1. **Males get worse grades than females in college (and in high school).**

   The average GPA for male high school graduates in 2000 in the United States was 2.83, while the average GPA for female high school graduates was 3.05.[1] There is no evidence this situation changes in higher education. For example, with information provided by the Office of the Vice President for Academic Affairs at Truman State University, the gender gap for seniors was 3.13 for men and 3.39 for women. For four classes over three years, not one class showed men's GPA equaling or even approaching the women's GPA.[2]

2. **The retention rate for male students in college is lower than that for female students.**

   Average retention rate for female students is around 66%, while it is only 59% for male students in college. Less than half of students admitted to college are males, and the lower retention rate means that even fewer will graduate.

3. **The percentage of college graduates who are males has declined for 30 years, and is now under 40% of graduates.**

   This is the real crux of the issue. If males were merely getting worse grades, the issue would not be as great. But there is a need for more male college graduates from a number of perspectives. Business requires more workers with a college education. Retirees and retirement plans counting on a healthy economy and stock market are dependent on a new generation of increasingly smart and productive workforce. For individuals and families, the benefits of a college education are increasingly apparent. Post-industrial societies such as the United States and Canada cannot compete effectively in a global economy with many of their smartest people unable to become professionals and knowledge workers.

4. As high school seniors, fewer boys expect to graduate from college than girls.
In 1980, the same percentage of boys and girls expected to complete college. Shortly thereafter, a gender gap began to appear and the gap grew steadily wider. By 1999, 60% of high school senior girls expected to complete college, while only 50% of high school senior boys expected to complete college, according to "The Gender Gap in College Expectations" by John Reynolds, Florida State University.[3]

Basically, there are 2 million smart young men missing from college every year. That is, there are 2 million boys not in college who test at the same or higher levels as girls who are currently enrolled in college. Educational Testing Service researchers Warren Willingham and Nancy S. Cole (former President of ETS) are quite direct when they write, "Based on a wide variety of tests and a number of large nationally representative samples of high school seniors, we see no evidence of any consequential difference in the average test performance of young women and men."[4]

The phenomenon began around 1980, and the graduation gap gradually grew wider so that by 2004 males were less than 40% of college graduates. The phenomenon is also international, occurring in most post-industrial advanced nations such as Canada, the United Kingdom, Australia and countries in Europe. It impacts families from upper socio-economic levels, and boys attending quality secondary schools as well.

Ruling out some theories.
There have been many theories as to why young men do worse than young women in college. Those theories include:
- Males are underachieving.
- Parents have lower expectations of their sons.
- An increase of low income and minority students in schools accounts for the problem.
- Dysfunctional families and social issues in families cause the problem.
- Parents are not raising their sons correctly.
- Boys are not behaving well.
- The problem is boys' lack of verbal skills.

• Since they mature later, males should attend college later in life. We can rule out these theories. Here is the evidence.

Males are not underachieving.

While males do get lower grades, they test at the same level as females. SAT scores as well as scores on a host of other tests show that males and females test at roughly the same levels.

Of note, there are two areas of gender difference in test scores. Males score higher in spatial tests than females, and females score higher in verbal and language skills. Males continue to earn higher average scores than females on ACT's mathematics and science tests, while females continue to earn higher average scores than males on the English and reading tests.[5]

Parental expectations are just as high.

While boys receive lower grades than girls in high school, parental expectations for boys remain as high as for girls. According to a study by Alan E. Marks, the Department of Psychology at Oglethorpe University, asked students "when you were in high school, in general, what was the lowest grade that your parents regarded as acceptable?" The mean average for boys was 2.50, and the mean average response for girls was 2.44, actually slightly lower than for boys.[6]

There is no connection with an increase of minority and low-income students.

The problem exists in other post-industrial societies where there are few minority students, such as New Zealand. The problem also exists in other post-industrial societies where there is much less inequality in wealth, such as Finland and Norway.

Parents raise their boys as well as their girls.

There is simply no documentation or research that indicates that parents raise their daughters with good academic habits, and then raise their sons with poor academic habits. Boys get lower GPAs even when their sisters do well in school. There is no indication precisely what parents do wrong in raising boys.

There is no connection with social problems in families.

The issue exists in two-parent traditional families. No study indicates that there is a gender difference with students from single-parent families.

Boys are behaving well.

All of the studies across time and generation indicate that boys behave better today than boys in previous generations. Compared to previous generations of young men, the crime rate is down, drug use down, and pregnancy rates (among other indicators) are down. There is no reporting from the work place that young men perform any worse than young women at work.

Boys need more verbal skills.

Females have better verbal skills than males because of their neurology. But this has always been the case, even when males were a majority of college students. For example, data from the University of Massachusetts at Amherst indicates that even when boys score higher on verbal SATs than girls, their GPAs are still lower.[7]

Maturity helps, but does not close the gap.

Males do mature later in life than females, with the average young man's brain now not fully developed until his mid-twenties. Older male students, and this is equally true of older female students, do better in college than young men still in their teen years. Unfortunately, the gender gap in graduation rates is wider for students older than age 25. So postponing college for males until their mid or late twenties, or even later, does not close the gender gap in graduation rates, as men are less likely to attend college as they grow older.

There are two solutions to helping males succeed. They are:

A. Grade all students based on learning and knowledge, not on behavior.

B. Teach male and female students differently, not the same.

Teaching Tips for Your Male Students

There are a number of tips, techniques and strategies you can incorporate in your teaching to help your male students learn more. Some of them will be easy, some hard; some can be immediately adopted, others will take awhile; some are very practical, others conceptual. Some of them will help your female students to learn more as well; others are pretty specific to your male students. None of the tips will hinder the learning of your female students.

From the list of hundreds of good teaching techniques, we have selected these for two reasons. Many were chosen because they are specific to helping male students learn. Others were chosen because, while they may be seen as "just good teaching" and be helpful to your female students as well, nevertheless they are so important in the learning of your male students that they need to be stressed here. It might be a bit difficult for even the most committed teacher to adopt them all. Choose those which apply to your discipline, your teaching, and your students. Enacting any of them will help your male students to learn more.

1. Visualize your young male student as two years younger.

In terms of brain development and neurological maturation, a young man in your class is two years younger than his age. So if you have a 20-year-old male, visualize his cognitive maturity level as comparable to an 18-year-old woman. Then reset your expectations accordingly.

2. Create abstract problem-solving and moral debates.

"Males like abstract arguments, philosophical conundrums, and moral debates about abstract principles," says educator and author Michael Gurian.[8] Create some exercises and assignments that involve abstract problem-solving, moral debates and other philosophical issues to engage your male students more.

3. Allow stress reducers during tests.

Allow all your students to be able to use stress reducers during tests. Music, with headphones, may be a stress reducer for some of your students. White noise might also help some students to concentrate better.

Having a pet in the classroom actually increases the test scores of all students. One training center in Ohio trains dogs to accompany autistic children to class, so that they can calm down and focus more during the class.

4. Allow choice of window or window-less room during tests.

National testing agencies allow some students with disabilities to choose whether they want to take a test in a room with, or without, a window. The physical environment impacts up to 25% of learning, according to a U.S. Department of Education study.

5. Show young male students how to fidget.

Eddie Ennels, instructor at Baltimore City Community College, says to teach young men how to fidget. Allowing male students to fiddle or fidget silently actually increases their ability to concentrate. Encourage your male students to doodle, squeeze a Nerf or 'stress' ball, or fidget silently. Men never grow out of the need to fidget.

6. Allow failure.

Failure is learning misspelled, says Laura Burkey.[9] Some educators say we only learn from failure, not success. Males will be more apt to fail at a given task than your female students. Allow failure, and give all your students a second or even third chance at tasks and assignments to redo their work and improve.

7. Imitate the work world.

Male students generally respond enthusiastically to "real work world" situations. Anytime you have an opportunity to frame or position an assignment in a more work world setting, do it. Sometimes that might mean actually engaging the work world; other times imitating it is sufficient. Consider assignments involving a project, apprenticeship situation, engagement with a mentor, interview with working people, supervision by business people, or other opportunity for your students to interact with a real work world environment.

8. Provide very detailed and specific instructions.

All your Generation Y students (those born 1980 to 1999) actually want and need very detailed and specific instructions. Whenever giving assignments, be far more detailed than you think is necessary.

Gen Y lives in a world with so many different meanings, so many different interpretations, and so many opportunities for misunderstanding. They interact with people from different cultures with different assumptions. As a result, they want and require a great deal of specificity.

9. Do not use cursive.

When communicating with students, especially young men, do not send messages in handwriting using cursive. Whether marking papers, writing on a blackboard, or even sending an email, do not use cursive. A decreasing number of your students are able to read or write in cursive. Boys began to drop writing and reading cursive several years before girls, but now many if not most of your students cannot read or write cursive adequately.

10. Consider typing instead of handwriting.

Handwriting takes considerably more time and energy. And handwriting uses certain muscles that may be strong and well developed for adults, but hardly ever used by younger generations accustomed to keyboarding.

For essays and other extensive writing assignments in class, consider allowing students to type instead of using handwriting.

11. Offer tough new challenges.

On occasion, give a tough new challenge or assignment. Make sure the assignment is intellectually tough, not merely busy work or time consuming work. Your male students will likely rise to the challenge and find the new challenge exciting and engaging.

12. Make expectations clear, and rewardable.

Make expectations for your course clear. Males are more likely to see expectations as single fixed points or hurdles for which they can say "done that." If expectations keep growing, goals keep receding, and success measured by ongoing continual work moves past a perceived goal, then your male students are likely to lose interest and feel there is less integrity in the expectations.

13. Make the first assignment easy.

Creating initial success helps to establish a positive self image and can-do mood in your students. Especially your male students need time to adjust to the new environment of your classroom, begin to feel comfortable, settle the limbic system of their brain, and then tackle the cognitive challenges ahead. Getting tough early may be intimidating, and an early sense of failure or being overwhelmed often cannot be made up by students later. A number of faculty have discovered that starting off with the most rigorous assignments often leads to lower retention, not higher retention.

14. Spend the first week creating a safe environment.

Online faculty experts, such as Dr. Mary Dereshiwsky, COI, of Northern Arizona University, indicate that spending the first week of an online course in creating a safe environment increases student involvement and discussion. The recommendation is from online course experiences of faculty, but it is equally applicable to the face-to-face classroom.

Lacking in social cues compared to their female colleagues, your male students are going to need more specific and obvious reassurances. Males also have to settle down the limbic system in their brains, feel unthreatened and consequently emotional comfortable, before they can learn.

15. The more student orientation the better.
The more time you spend in student orientation, the better. So says online faculty authority Dr. Rita Conrad of Florida State University. Courses in which faculty spend more time in student orientation have greater retention of students. This finding is based on online courses, but can easily been seen to be relevant for traditional classroom teaching as well. There is technical orientation, logistical orientation, behavior or process orientation, and of course subject orientation.

16. Every 15–20 minutes, have some physical activity.
For the traditional classroom, all students benefit from a little physical activity 1-3 times during the class period. But your male students need that physical activity even more to help them concentrate and learn.

Every 15-20 minutes, have some physical activity that takes only 1-3 minutes. Some examples:

- Turn to your neighbor and ask her/him …..
- Rearrange the chairs (for small group discussions, or some other activity)
- Have your students stand up while you make a particularly important point.
- During question time, have each student toss a small Nerf ball to the next student asking a question.
- Have students stand up and take a seat somewhere else in the classroom.

17. Ask male students for tech help.
This is a win-win technique. Some of your male students will be nerds and techies. Asking them for tech help with your course engages them and solicits their commitment, demonstrates to other male students you value their expertise, and you actually gain some online tech help that will enhance your course. The biggest benefit is that it makes a statement from you as teacher that you value your male students and their contributions.

18. Use simulations and animations.

All Gen Y students learn more with simulations and animations, but the engagement and interaction is particularly helpful to the learning of your male students. Whether the simulations and animations are created by you, or you obtain permission to use them from their creator, consider them for as many units of your course as possible.

19. Try drag-and-drop exercises.

Drag-and-drop exercises have been proven to be an excellent learning tool. Online expert Bill Horton of Denver says that when students do drag-and-drop exercises with the cursor, they learn more than if they just heard or read the same information.

20. Offer challenges to find resources.

Consider challenging your students to find other simulations, animations and drag-and-drop exercises relevant for your course. More of your male students will tend to take you up on your challenge, resulting again in more engagement, commitment, and learning.

21. Revise discussion rubrics.

Discussion rubrics are criteria for how you score discussion. They were invented for online discussion, but you can create a rubric for in-person discussion as well. The rubric gives your students criteria so they know what a valuable comment is. It also gives you a guideline for establishing gender-neutral scoring of discussion.

22. Have a weekly surprise.

Mary Dereshiwsky of Northern Arizona University has developed a technique of offering a weekly surprise in her online classroom. Whether it is a poll, a treat, a trivia question, or some other surprise, the technique creates a level of expectation and interest for your students each and every time they come back to your online classroom.

23. Praise initially and subtly.

Initial praise goes a long way in motivating your male students. When that praise is made in front of the rest of the class, either in the online or physical classroom, make that praise more subtle and less overt. Here's an example of subtle praise: "So Tomas asks a good question, what do the rest of you think about that?" Here's an example of overt and over-the-top praise that can subject the male student to embarrassment and even ridicule from others - an example of too much praise: "Wow Tomas, terrific insight!" Note that we indicate that the same words of praise would be quite appropriate when delivered privately one-on-one with the male student.

24. Offer rewards.

Offered sporadically and unexpectedly, rewards enliven the class atmosphere, keep students stimulated, and motivate some of your male students. Rewards should almost always be minimal and token, including candy, small toys, pictures, links to fun web sites, and minor privileges. The rewards actually benefit the learning of all your students, not just those 'winning.'

25. Never punish.

You might fail to reward, but do not resort to punishment. Punishment is probably the biggest disincentive and inhibitor of learning in our business. If you must do something, instead of punishing some students, reward others for their good work. Punishment will lower your retention rate, turn off students, and create a level of fear that you do not want in your classroom. It is not just those students who get punished that suffer, as other students will be negatively affected as well.

26. Do not be negative.

Be positive. Be overly positive. Being enthusiastic and positive reinforces learning and helps everyone in your class. Be aware of how your students might perceive your words and actions, as their perceptions may be very different for your intentions. You might not think you are being negative, but your students might. Studies indicate that you and I think we are smiling most of the time, when film shows we are only smiling a very small part of the time. So your perception is not the "right" one; your students' perceptions are what matter.

If you do not think of yourself as having a personality of enthusiasm, then consider creating an alter ego, a second identity, one in which you are enthusiastic and positive. Remember, this is not about you. It is about helping your students learn more. We're positive you can do it!

27. Expect high-level performance.

Australian professor Philip C. Candy, in his book *Self Direction for Lifelong Learning,* says: "Educators who hold high expectations for their students tend to convey these through complex and subtle patterns of interaction, which commonly result in the learners living up to these expectations, and in the process, developing a more positive image of themselves."[(10)]

28. Provide help with frustration.

Male students may be more apt to experience frustration in your course. When the learner is unhappy about some situation, focus on how the student feels about the situation, not the situation itself. Listen fully, try not to provide the answer or make a point, and sympathize with the person's point of view, even if you don't agree with it.

When a student expresses frustration:

a) Don't contradict the person's views.

b) Don't use logical explanations.

c) Don't ridicule the person's view.

d) Convey your positive regard for the person.[(11)]

29. Never be overcome by emotion.

It is fine to express emotion. It is great to be passionate. But when your emotion overtakes you, pause, take some deep breaths, and do not be overcome by your emotions. For male students with fewer emotional tools to draw upon, your emotional response may be reframed as a threat or aggression, which is the cue to turn off the cognitive brain for a male.[(12)]

30. Be wrong.

One of the most successful teaching techniques with male students is to give in over a minor point to get past an argument or mental block. You can say you are wrong, or admit you don't know, or offer a compromise statement like "I had not thought of that," or "I didn't think of it that way."

In terms of learning, the technique allows the student to 'win the battle' while you 'win the war' in terms of the student accepting or learning the larger or bigger point. Internally, it allows the student to think or do it 'his own way' and yet to reach the same conclusion as you (the teacher) wish him to reach.

31. Do not threaten, even humorously.

The college classroom is one of the most stressful places and times in their life for most male students. In a study of Carleton College alumni recollections, recent nightmares about college was the most common alumni experience provoking memories of student life.[13] Do not threaten, even humorously. There is no humor in it for a young male student.

32. Utilize virtual worlds.
Virtual worlds like Second Life give your male students a chance to exercise their spatial skills, as well as role play in a "real" world situation. Consider creating an assignment in a virtual world. Have an adjunct instructor, graduate student or a student in your class monitor or create the assignment if you are not familiar with virtual worlds.

For Gen Y the virtual world is a real world, and many of your students will actually either make a living, or make their work more productive or profitable, by using a virtual world to enhance their work in the physical world.

33. Have your students create content.
It is said that over half of teenagers have already created content on the web. For Gen Y, they are not just consumers of information on the web; they are also producers of information on the web. When given the challenge to create content for your course, your students are likely to be more involved and committed, and to learn more.

34. Offer pre-course quizzes.
Male students are particularly goal or benchmark-oriented. They want to know where they stand, and where they need to be. Pre-course quizzes help all your students to establish a beginning knowledge benchmark, from which they can gauge their learning during your course. Pre-course quizzes also help you to know what areas your students need more help in, and where they are already proficient.

35. Adopt video games.
Allow and encourage male students to play computer games and online games. Explore whether an assignment could involve playing a video game. Video and online gaming is almost certainly an important work skill that your students will use in their professional work. For example, Dr. James Rosser, a surgeon, plays video games between surgeries. He did a study of other doctors who play video games and found that surgeons who play video games make 37% fewer mistakes

than surgeons who do not play video games.[14]

36. Understand young men's peak learning times.

Every person has a peak learning time. And it is not the same hours of the day for everyone. Many young men do not learn as much in early morning classes, and learn more in the afternoon, evening, and even late at night. In fact, one study found that 20% of all adult employees work best in the evening, and 6% are most productive overnight.

Take into consideration peak learning time when holding classes, presentations and giving exams.

37. Have them teach each other.

Probably the most effective learning strategy ever devised is to have the learner teach someone else. By having your better students do peer teaching and sharing with others in your class, both those teaching and those learning will increase their knowledge and expertise. In peer teaching, other students will likely also have a different style that will complement that of your teaching style, thus enhancing the ability of your students to learn more.

38. Provide ungraded self-quizzes.

Ungraded self-quizzes, a built-in feature of most online classrooms, are a new tool that students almost universally praise for one reason: immediate feedback. Students like to receive immediate feedback, because it gives them instant analysis of where they stand and what they have achieved. Ungraded quizzes are popular because there is no penalty and thus no stress for students. By creating ungraded self-quizzes for each unit of your course, you create immediate feedback on your students' learning without taking any of your time to score the quizzes.

39. Is there anything I should know?

Ask one question at the beginning of every new course. Ask each student, in a way in which his or her response can be private, "Is there anything I should know about you that will help you learn more?" A good way is to have this question on a sheet of paper or an email, so that the student's response will be confidential. One professor reported a young man in her class then confessed he was hard of hearing in one ear, telling her he had never told any other teacher about it. From then on, the professor made sure she stood where he was able to hear her during the course.

40. Add one of your own.
If you are able to send it to us, do so by emailing it to the authors at draves@lern.org.

Pick and choose which of the above work for you and your students. You are a professional teacher. Some may not fit your style. There are some of them with which you may violently disagree. And one of these tips is probably just plain wrong. But the vast majority of these ideas have been proven to be effective, and are cited by more than one teaching authority. And at least one of them, we are sure, will make a big and positive difference for your male students.

Why boys do less work

Probably the two greatest learning and work issues for faculty with respect to male students are:

- Male students are far more likely to turn work in late.
- Male students, in general, do less course work than female students.

The most important thing for faculty to understand is that while males may turn in work late and do less course work, they test the same as female students.[15] That is, males learn the same amount and gain the same amount of knowledge as their female counterparts.

Male students get worse grades than female students. This begins at or before the sixth grade, and continues right through to the senior year in college. There is no closing of the gender gap.

From our research and work, we have determined that the gender gap in GPA is due to the twin issues of males turning work in late and doing less work. For instance, in a survey of teachers some 84% of teachers say that boys turn work in late more often than girls. Individual case studies of class scores on homework confirm this.

Most of the research on course work involves secondary education, where norm-referenced test scores administered by external testing agencies can be compared with grades and homework time. However, there is no evidence that the issues of male students in college are any different from the issues of male students in high school. Our educational system is essentially the same from secondary through undergraduate study, with the same grading criteria and the same experience in gender discrepancies, and the same experiences and problems being reported by higher education faculty and secondary school teachers.

"Gender Difference and Student Learning," an important study done by Dr. Yi Du, Ph.D., Director of Research and Evaluation at the Edina, Minnesota, public schools statistically documents that girls do more homework than boys. The Edina study found that in grades 8 through 12, significantly more females reported spending at least one hour doing homework daily than males. Females in grade 9 and 12 outnumbered males in spending three hours doing homework daily across four years. In the junior year of high school, the study reports males did about one-third less homework and as seniors males did just one-half of the homework that female students did.[16]

Sue Hallam of the University of London, working with Lynne Rogers of the Open University in the United Kingdom, also studied the gender differences in approaches to studying among high-achieving students. Rogers and Hallam found that "the boys reported doing less homework than the girls."[17]

Writing in *Educational Psychology,* Jianzhong Xu also found that girls do more homework, reporting that girls "reported that they spent more time doing homework, were less likely to come to class without homework, and considered homework less boring."[18]

We received an email from a high school boy who reported that he works 16 hours a week, does no homework, and studies about four hours for every test. This illustrates the behavior of literally millions of other male students. We know:

Males are oriented to the workplace. This student, and male workers in general, must report to work on time and must do an adequate amount of work, as he continues to have a job that is almost half-time.

Males are not oriented to homework. This student, and male students in general, does less homework than females.

Males are oriented towards tests. This student, and male students in general, studies for the test.

All of the research shows that males and females approach homework and coursework differently.

Educators at the University of Southampton in the United Kingdom studied why boys do worse on homework than girls, and found that boys often 'batch' their time, so they will work less frequently on homework, while girls will work more consistently and steadily. This could be part of the explanation as to why more boys than girls turn in homework late. Females work more regularly and consistently, while males tend more than females to work in spurts, separated by periods of rest.

It may be that the neurological reason behind the 'batching' of time for males is based on the male need for more brain rest, and more frequent brain resting. This would be consistent with another of the findings of the University of Southampton researchers.

They also found that males often view "home" and "work" as very separate. That is, work takes place outside of the home, while home is a place to rest and not do work. We know that historically male work has primarily taken place outside of the house. Females, by contrast, apparently do not place such a dichotomy between home and work, and do not view them as opposites or contradictory, say the University of Southampton researchers.

Rogers and Hallam suggest that boys study differently, and use time more effectively, than girls. "The findings suggest that overall, high-achieving boys have better studying strategies than high-achieving girls. They achieve high standards while doing less homework."[19]

Jianzhong Xu provides more supportive conclusions. "Compared with boys, girls more frequently reported working to manage their workspace, budget their time, and monitor their emotions."[20] While the conclusion of the Xu study appears at odds with the conclusion of the Rogers and Hallam research about study habits, they both have in common the finding that girls and boys approach and do home-work differently. We suggest that both conclusions are consistent and true. That is, females' approach to homework yields greater success in completing homework, while males' approach to homework yields greater time-efficiency and knowledge acquisition in preparing for tests and exams. Females are studying to get good homework and course grades, which they do; while males are studying to get good test and exam scores, which they do.

All students want more challenge.

Surveys of students of both sexes indicate that their biggest problem with school is that it is not challenging enough, with 85% of students describing secondary schooling as "boring." Thus, it is important to distinguish between the quantity of work required for students to do, and the quality or level of challenge required for students. More work does not equal more challenge.

Male students are far more likely to view attaining a level of learning and knowledge as a hurdle to be jumped over - once.

And after attaining that learning or knowledge, they are more likely to want to move on to a new challenge.

For example, if you asked your students to add 2 + 2 some 100 times and turn it in, your female students would think it a stupid exercise but they would do it. Your male students, however, would be very likely to simply refuse to do it, no matter what the consequence.

Smart male students often simply reject or refuse to do work which they regard as busy work. "I preferred to endure all sorts of punishments rather than learn gabble by rote," is how Albert Einstein as a student phrased it.[21] Steve Jobs, founder of Apple Computer, noted that as a university student "after six months I couldn't see the value in it."[22] Einstein and Jobs are representative of millions of male students in college every year.

In fact, males are motivated by new challenges, where females are far less so. Utah State University instructor Jennie Chamberlain once experimented in her class by giving homework to students for a chapter they had yet to read or cover in class. All of the boys completed and turned the homework on time, while many of the girls had problems doing work that had not yet been covered in class, she reported.[23]

Males will accept punishment.

When they feel something is stupid or wrong or a waste of time, males tend to accept punishment rather than change their behavior.

Julie Jorgensen, a mother and CEO of her own company, decided with her husband that they would penalize their son for late homework by taking something out of his bedroom each time he turned in his work late. After two weeks, the only things left in his bedroom were his bed and his books, Ms. Jorgensen reported.[24]

Boys are not lazy and unmotivated.

Like teachers did 100 years ago, today many faculty members believe that boys and young men are lazy and unmotivated.

This is not the first generation of males to have this charge leveled at them. From a historical perspective, it would, however, be the first time the charge has held up to be true.

Let's look at the evidence.

- Young men in the military have not been reported to be lazy and unmotivated by their commanders.
- Boys, as a gender, have not been reported to be lazy and unmo-

tivated at work by employers. All employers would like all their employees to be more motivated and energetic, but compared to females, no employers report that boys or male workers are less motivated or less energetic.

- Male sports teams do not perform any less well now than female sports teams.
- Even the crime rate for males in the mid 1990s to mid 2000s is reported to be down over previous generations of boys.
- Boys test equally with girls.

Only in the academic setting are boys and young men said to be lazy and unmotivated. Even in school boys test equally with girls in almost all areas except language, keeping in mind that males have never had higher language skills than females.

Boys and young men do "appear" to be lazy and unmotivated in class. For example:

- Boys and young males either have higher incidences of Attention Deficit Hyperactivity Disorder (ADHD) and autism, or we have identified more cases of ADHD and autism than ever before.
- A greater percentage of boys and young males receive medication than any previous generation.
- Like the generation of their great grandfathers 100 years ago, they exhibit a measure of wandering and exploring and seeming lack of purpose as they encounter an entirely new economic and technological age.
- Boys today almost surely mature at a rate that is slower and takes longer than previous generations, resulting in maturity that does not arrive until the mid to late -20s.
- Boys today, and to an extent girls in Generation Y, are - and perceive themselves to be - more socially awkward than previous generations.
- Girls today, like their great grandmothers 100 years ago, are perceived by the media to be more talented, smarter and more assertive than boys.
- There are clearly more boys than girls at the low end of the intelligence and academic achievement spectrums; and presumably more on the lower end of the motivation spectrum as well.
- And they definitely like to play more than girls. As we have noted elsewhere, all young primate males play more than young female primates. This is certainly not a recent trend.

We do know that all generations of youth are judged to be less able by their elders. John Willetts, who served in the U.S. military during World War II, told us that in 1939 his generation was publicly regarded as physically unfit and inadequate for adulthood. Less than two years later, his generation was of course saving democracy and creating the "greatest generation" label for itself.

We do know that the new technology, the transition from one economy to another, the ADHD, autism, medication, slower brain development and maturation rate, social awkwardness, and need to play more than girls all are realities "in play" for male students today. They certainly contribute to the appearance in the classroom and in the academic institution of being lazy and unmotivated. We suggest however, that the facts demonstrate otherwise.

We suggest that male students in fact are performing at the same level academically as female students, as demonstrated by their test scores and performance in the work place. We also suggest that if we as faculty have or exhibit preconceived notions of laziness or lack of motivation, male students will not respond positively to our teaching.

The twin issues of doing less work and turning in work late are not attitudinal or a willing disrespect or neglect on the part of your male students. It is most likely hard-wired. The statistical prevalence of the numbers across time and across societies is so substantial that there is no other conclusion that can be reached.

Punishment in most cases does not work. We know that because most faculty and teachers punish late and incomplete work with lower grades, and yet the gender gap in GPA never closes or even narrows.

The most important thing for faculty to understand is that while males may turn in work late and do less course work, they test the same as female students. That is, males learn the same amount and gain the same amount of knowledge as their female counterparts.

Chapter 13.
Helping Female students learn more

Gender is clearly one of the important early entry issues into moving from the factory model of teaching to the personalised teaching of the 21st century.

In the current factory model, we treat female students the same as male students, and vice versa. Yet we know that female students learn differently, test differently, have different abilities when it comes to spatial and language skills, and have different neurological and hormonal brain structures.

While there are issues with how male students are treated in school and college, the issues with female students are different, and no less fascinating. The issues with female students point out the inherent weakness of the factory model of teaching.

There are two major challenges with female students in schools and colleges today. The first challenge with female students is that while young women get better grades than young men and even study more than male students, they do not learn more. The second challenge is that there is evidence that schools and colleges promote work habits that actually hinder women in the workplace.

With respect to the first challenge, at first glance it would seem that female students should have higher academic achievement than male students given that they receive better grades, have higher retention rates in college, and are admitted to and graduate in higher numbers than males. But they do not have higher academic achievement.

Apparently, the factory model of teaching, biased as it is towards female students, does not help female students learn more.

In this chapter we explore why female students do not learn more than male students, and suggest some innovative ideas for helping girls, young women, and women learn more. Then we address the issue of gender pay equity in the workplace and offer some evidence that schools and colleges promote work habits that actually hinder women in the workplace.

We will refer to female students variously as girls, young women and women, but these terms do not indicate any meaning other than possible differences in maturation and age, as illustrated by the evidence that girls' brains do not mature fully until their early twenties.

Terminology for females is very generational in nature. For senior citizens, the word "girls" is used to describe women of any age. For women of the World War II generation, the word "girls" is a term of respect, and one which they use to refer to each other. For Baby Boomer women, however, the term "girls" is perceived negatively as a demeaning term. Generation X women appear to embrace and/or accept a variety of terms, none of which appear to be demeaning. And Generation Y, which in a number of interesting ways is similar to the senior citizens of the World War II generation, also appears to use the term "girls." As authors, we have no preference nor are we trying to convey any subtle message other than occasionally be more precise (such as young women versus women) or more varied in our use of language from the somewhat academic terminology of "female students," a term apparently no generation embraces in common usage.

As we have stated in other chapters, males and females are overall equally intelligent. Males and females differ in ability in two areas: males have higher spatial ability and females have higher language ability. Male and female students overall test equally. Male students do not test as well as females in language areas. Female students do not test as well as males in spatial ability.

This testing difference has existed for decades, during times of gender bias against females, times when females have been a minority of students, and during the last 30 years when females have been in the majority of college graduates. Susan Pinker writes that Dr. Doreen Kimura, Canadian neuroscientist, Simon Fraser University, and the researcher who proved that testosterone difference explains spatial ability between the sexes, is "baffled as to how any serious scientist could deny the biological triggers of male-female differences."[1]

Female students get better grades because they are graded on their behavior, and the desired behavior is more characteristic of female neurology than male neurology. When others say that female students have better or higher "academic achievement," they are referring to grades, not test scores.

Why do girls study more?

Studies done by Dr. Yu of Edina School District and others indicate that female students study more than male students. A Canadian study agrees, saying about males that "They hand in less homework, are less likely to get along with teachers, and are less interested in what they are learning in class."[2]

The estimates vary, and they also vary in K-12 education by grade level, with seniors in high school having the largest discrepancy. We use a percentage cited in the Edina study of 30% as a reasonable discrepancy. It is clearly not 5% and not 70%, so the number also is one that indicates the relative difference in a visual or image sense.

Do female students study more than male students because they need the extra time to learn the same amount of material, or do they do it for another reason? There is no research concluding that females need to study more than males to acquire the same learning and knowledge. Coates suggests that smart females do not need to study more than males, and that females study more than males to please the instructor and get good grades. She suggests that at some point smart females will also begin to view the extra time spent on homework and coursework as wasted time, and points to some anecdotal evidence that this is beginning to happen with smart female students.

The empathy factor

The implications of Susan Pinker's work suggest that female students, possessing a neurology and hormonal make up that results in more empathy than males, is also a reason why female students study more. That is, female students want to please the instructor, because that pleases the student, and quite possibly, Pinker infers, there is an internal hormonal reward in additional ocytocin for female students.

Pinker writes, "Women, on average, showed more activity in the more recently evolved part of the limbic system, the cingulated gyrus (where Tania Singer found evidence of individual differences in empathic reactions to pain in others)."[3]

The work of Simon Baron-Cohen provides a biological explanation for why females rank meaningful work and contributing to the benefit of others so highly, and power and money lower on their list of goals than males do.[4]

The empathy factor is also a logical explanation why more women become primary care physicians than laprodopic surgeons, a type of surgery which involves spatial ability and where male doctors predominate. It is a logical explanation as to why more female veterinary students go into small pet practice with cats and dogs than in large or food animal veterinary medicine.

Gender equity in the workplace

The second major challenge for schools and colleges with respect to female students is that the factory model of school may not be preparing female students adequately for the workplace.   While women are doing well in school, there are still gender equity issues, especially equal pay for the same job, in the workplace.

There is no evidence that giving women an advantage in school has led to greater pay equity in the workplace. Females have always had better grades in school than males.

And while the percentage of male graduates has been declining since 1980, the "glass ceiling" or gender pay gap stopped closing around the mid 1990s, with some exceptions, thus showing no relationship between keeping males from graduating and closing the gender pay gap.

Indeed, Sweden, the nation that has closed the gender pay gap the most, does not attribute its success to anything related to education. Instead, Swedish women attribute the narrowing of the gender pay gap to paternity leave, maternity leave, and a law requiring half of its local and nationally elected officials to be women.

Thus, favoring female students in education does not appear to help in closing the gender pay gap for women in the workplace.

The 5 bad learning habits for women

There is evidence that suggests that female students acquire bad learning habits in school that hurt their work, productivity and success in the work world.

These negative work world traits are rewarded and reinforced by schools, colleges and universities. In her book, "New Girl on the Job," author Hannah Seligson defines five bad work habits of women, all of which are rewarded and reinforced by schools. The five bad work habits are:

1. Perfection

"Women are more likely to define competence as perfection," writes Seligson. (5) She suggests in the workplace that competence - getting a job done and then moving on - is more productive and profitable for one's employer than perfection.

2. Lack of priority

For too many women, everything is important. "You just need to get 80% of everything done" maintains Seligson, who interviewed over 100 successful career women on why many women do not do as well as men on the job. (6)

3. Too detailed

Women focus too much on details. Minor details often have little or no effect on profitability, often taking up too much time and costing money. In the work place, a focus on major items rather than details is most often more valuable.

4. Failure seen as bad

Failure in the work place is, and should be, seen as an important avenue to success. Making mistakes is not the same as underperformance. Underperformance is consistent. Making mistakes, especially for the first time, is common and acceptable. Superior workers make mistakes. Managers and leaders in the workplace make big mistakes. It is just that superior workers and profitable leaders do not make the same mistakes, nor consistent mistakes. They learn from mistakes and then create success.

5. Work martyr

Seligson says that too many women feel an obligation to be the last one to leave the office. That often leads to an expectation that the woman will be the last one to leave the office, and then to the delegation of extra non-essential work.

The combination of being a work martyr, being focused on details and perfection with a lesser sense of priority, makes for an employee who is not as productive, profitable or successful, concludes Seligson.

Innovative ideas for helping women learn more

Your authors maintain that all of these bad work habits named by Seligson originate as bad learning habits, formed, reinforced and rewarded by schools.

We suggest these innovative ideas for helping female students to both learn more, and acquire better work habits that will be rewarded more in the work place.

1. Revise homework and coursework to pass/fail.

Homework and coursework grading should be revised to pass/fail to devalue the perfection of an 'A.' There is nothing wrong with excellence or getting a perfect score. But it is required neither in school nor in the workplace. Excellence should be measured by the level of academic challenge achieved, not by the perfection of lesser academic challenges.

2. Challenge female students to spend less time per module, and to tackle more challenging modules.

Female students should be spending less time studying per module or unit of material. For example, Coates has found research that Israeli women take the lowest level of math to qualify for engineering or high tech jobs in college. They do better than men on the low levels of math competency. They could do well in higher-level math, but make lower grades. So female students choose to do better on low-level material than to do adequately on higher-level knowledge. This choice, the study concludes, limits the future options of smart female students.

Instead, smart female students should be challenged to tackle more challenging work. Female students should reallocate valuable time from repetitive work that does not result in any greater learning or knowledge to spending that valuable time on more challenging material which does lead to greater learning and knowledge. This is not difficult to do, and teachers can accomplish this by rewarding passing harder tests more than getting 'A's on easier work.

3. Do not reward behavior.

Female students should not be rewarded for behavior, such as turning work in on time. This behavior is almost certainly a function of neurology rather than conscious will. Women do not fidget as often as men because they have 15% more serotonin, not because they are more responsible.

Rewarding behavior has numerous negative consequences for female students.

It tells many female students they know something when in fact they do not.

Teachers and schools should not tell a female student she knows a given level of knowledge when she does not.

Willingham and Cole report that about 30% of female students and just 20% of male students get significantly higher grades than their test scores would indicate. At the extremities, for students with extremely high grades and very low test scores, the gender difference is even more pronounced, with far more females than males.

One female college instructor reflected, "We have two goddaughters in Texas who, on paper, are doing quite well in school. One of them will graduate from high school with a B- C report card, and she's quite frankly functionally illiterate in both math, writing and basically anything you would consider academic. But her grades do not reflect it. She is a very nice child - she attends every day and turns her work in on time - but basically has not learned anything in three years. And that's scary, that's very scary."[7]

It is difficult to make up a knowledge gap when a student does not know it exists.

Giving students good grades when they have not learned the material sufficiently masks academic achievement. The student will not know to make up a knowledge gap, because there is no way to identify that knowledge gap.

Telling female students they know something when they do not hinders them in the workplace.

They will reasonably expect more rewards in the workplace than they may qualify for. And they may be confused by the reward system in the workplace that is different from that in school. In most work places involving knowledge jobs, employers do not consider attendance and turning work in on time as sufficient for reward, such as raises and promotions.

4. Reward failure.

Teachers often reward elementary school children for failure, and are to be commended for that (as well as many other positive pedagogical practices elementary school teachers employ).

But from middle school through higher education, failure is rarely rewarded. This is of particular concern for female students, because females tend to be risk averse and lower risk-takers than males in general.

There are good biological and evolutionary reasons why females over the past 10,000 years have been more reluctant to take risks. Taking care of infants, historically the role of the mother, is not the place where one usually should experiment. Preventing risk with young ones more likely will lead to their achieving adulthood.

But in today's work place, risk is a prerequisite to innovation and invention. Failure often leads to success.

Teachers at all levels should reward failure by offering and encouraging the following:

Re-taking of tests, so that students can retake quizzes and tests over and over again until the material is learned;

Reworking of papers and other homework and coursework, so that all students can improve upon their work by redoing it. This should be done not just for failing work, but even or especially for passing or average work.

Quizzing out of tests. Allowing and encouraging all students to try to quiz out of a test encourages them to move up academically to higher and more challenging levels of study.

Ways to Teach Girls Differently

From a workshop we did for teachers, here are the top ways the participants suggested to help girls learn more. Notice they are a combination of a) emphasizing female strengths and at the same time b) assisting them with those areas where females generally have more difficulty than males.

1. Give lots of practice with multiple choice tests.

Female students do not do as well as male students on multiple-choice tests. Give them more practice with multiple-choice tests.

2. Move on to a challenge; spend less time on what they already know.

Female students will benefit from more challenges, and especially new challenges. When a female student has accomplished or mastered a given area of learning and knowledge, move that student on to more difficult material. In Israel, for example, girls enrolled in the lowest level of math necessary to qualify for studying science and engineering, although they could have been successful with more demanding courses.[8]

3. Measure how long you can be on a task.

Female students are able to stay on a task longer than male students before needing a break, but even females benefit from mental and/or physical breaks every 15-20 minutes. Be sure to provide plenty of breaks to maximize attention and retention.

4. More small group work time.

Females tend to learn more by interacting with others in a group setting. Females often learn by the process of communication, and discussion is one way women learn.

5. More oral presentations.

Females in general have good communication skills, so oral presentations are a good way for female students to share what they know.

6. Provide indirect lighting.

Your female students will be able to focus better with indirect lighting, while your male students need more light and more overhead light.

7. More hands-on manipulative exercises for spatial ability.

Females do not have as good a spatial ability as males, so more hands-on practice and manipulation for spatial ability might assist them in this skill area.

8. Engage in less competition.

While males learn more in a mildly competitive situation, females learn more by working together on the same team rather than in a competitive situation.

Women in STEM

We should welcome and invite, but not demand, female students to enter science, technical, engineering and math (STEM), as practicing professionals. And we should not expect female students to enter the STEM professions in the same proportion as male students.

To be sure, every female who wants to enter a STEM profession should not only be encouraged but assisted in every way. We have a shortage of professionals in the STEM areas. But equally, every male who wants to enter a STEM profession should also be encouraged and assisted in every way.

There are three considerations why we should not expect the proportion of females to significantly exceed 20% of STEM professionals.

Females in STEM have not grown significantly.

The first reason is that while females are a greater proportion of college graduates for the last thirty years, they have not become a significantly greater proportion of practicing STEM professionals.

A study in the United Kingdom showed that while males entered the STEM fields in fewer numbers, the percentage of women in those fields did not increase over time.[9]

Pinker notes that women are 2.8 times more likely than men to leave science and engineering careers, despite the study by Catherine Weinberger that has shown that women with computer science or engineering degrees earn 30 to 50 percent more than the average female graduate.[10]

When the United States issues a special H1-B visa to skilled STEM workers in other countries to come to the United States, some 73% of those H1-B visa workers are college-educated males, not females. These professions include nursing, so the male percentage without nursing would be even higher.[11]

Also contributing is the fact that many of the female PhDs who enter scientific fields leave soon after they begin working. A study by the *Chronicle of Higher Education* found that 75% of female STEM graduates become teachers, not practicing professionals in science, technology, engineering or math. By contrast only 25% of male STEM graduates decide not to practice.

A 1995 survey of Americans with PhDs in science, technology, engineering, and mathematics found that single men and single women with PhDs participate about equally in the scientific workforce. But a married female PhD is 11 percent less likely to work full time than a married male PhD. If the woman is married with young children, then she is 25 percent less likely to be fully employed in science or technology than a married man with young children.[12]

There are neurological considerations.

One line of reasoning suggests there are neurological factors as to why females might not constitute more than around 20% of STEM practitioners in the post-industrial world. The 20% benchmark comes from Michael Gurian's work suggesting there are about 20% of members of either sex with a gender characteristic of the other sex, a benchmark that appears to receive some confirmation by the percentage of women in many STEM professions.

Those neurological considerations have already been reviewed, and include the lower spatial ability of most females due to a lower testerone level than males, a higher verbal and communication ability than males, and a greater tendency towards empathy than males. As Doreen Kimura notes, "In normal young men and women, spatial ability is systematically related to testosterone (T) levels."[13]

Women may not want to enter STEM.

The third consideration is clearly the most interesting, which is that women may not choose to enter STEM professions in the same proportion as men.

Pinker states, "the richer the country, the more likely women and men choose different types of jobs." Coates also found that the percentage of engineers who were women varied by country based on the level of democracy and economic prosperity of the country. In less democratic and less economically prosperous countries, the proportion of female engineers was greater than 20%. This was true for Bulgaria (50%), East Germany (28%) and the Arab Sector of Israel (50%). In more prosperous and democratic countries, the proportion of female engineers was lower, around 20%. This was true for the United States (20%), United Kingdom (18%), Western Europe (21%) and the Jewish Sector of Israel (28%).

Interestingly, when East Germany merged with West Germany the proportion of female engineers in eastern Germany dropped from 50% down to the proportion in the former West Germany.[14]

Coates also found that programs encouraging elementary and secondary school-age girls to become practicing STEM professionals had little impact. One such study of Camp Reach, a middle-school engineering outreach program for girls concluded, "While a higher fraction of the Camp Reach group chose engineering majors upon college entry, the difference did not reach statistical significance. There were no significant differences in the engineering self-efficacy and other measures of efficacy between the Reach and control groups."
[15]

Instead of expecting women to perform the same with respect to science, technology, engineering and math professions as men, understanding gender differences between males and females offers education an opportunity to maximize the skills and strengths of all our students.

Pinker offers the conclusion, "There is new evidence that it is a good idea to trust women's choices instead of pushing them to study what doesn't appeal to them."

Chapter 14.
Students with Asperger's and Autism

A few years ago, it was uncommon to have autistic students in the classroom. Asperger's Syndrome was something that was considered rare, and few people knew about it. Today, there are growing numbers of students in the K-12 system who are affected by autism disorders or other neurologically based differences that impact how they learn - and consequently, how teachers must operate in order to be successful. Traditional notions of "good pedagogy" may be not only ineffective, but even detrimental to some of today's students.

No one is normal

"The last thing that man will understand in nature is the performance of his brain." John C. Eccles (quoted by C.C. Pfeiffer in *Mental and Elemental Nutrients,* 1975)

The brain is the most mysterious of all organs. It is the command center for our physical, spiritual, emotional, and intellectual existence. In the past 25 years, neuroscientists have discovered more about the brain than we had understood in the preceding 10,000 years, and yet there is still much to learn about how the brain functions, and how the human brain develops.

In many religious traditions, there is a set age at which people are believed to be sufficiently mature of mind to be held accountable as adults for their actions. These ages vary widely. In the Catholic tradition, for example, the age of seven was considered the age of accountability or the age of reason. In Judaism, young people are welcomed to adulthood with a Bar Mitzvah or a Bat Mitzvah at the age of 13. Regardless of the age at which children were considered to be of adult mind, the basic premise was the same. There is an age at which children are mentally mature enough to act as an adult would act and to be held accountable by adult rules, and that age is the same for everyone.

Neuroscientists now know that the development of the brain is far more complex than could have been imagined in past centuries. Not only are there structural gender differences, but we now know that the brain matures in different sequences related to gender, and at different rates. We also know that prenatal exposure to hormones influences the function of the brain for life. Scientists have learned a great deal in the last two decades about the role and function of different areas of the brain and about the effects of experience on brain development. A great deal more is also known about how neurological differences may affect brain development and the rate at which the brain becomes "mature." While these differences may be unrelated to intelligence, they are very much related to behavior, and this is often equated with intellectual ability in school.

There are some key points about the brain that have become much more important to educators.

- *The brain is plastic.* It is a responsive organ and its function can be impacted or changed by experience.
- *The brain is adaptive.* The main function of the brain is the survival of the organism, and the brain adapts to the environment of the individual in ways to maximize survival.
- *Every brain is unique.* Every individual has unique experiences which affect their mental processes, and thus, every individual thinks, learns, and behaves in a unique way.

In the past, both scientists and society as a whole have tended to think of the brain in simple terms. Either a person was "normal" or "abnormal," adequate or deficient. More recently, neuroscientists have begun to use a different term - "neurotypical" - to describe the neurological behavior that is most characteristic of people in society. For those who have neurological differences, there is a move away from the medical model of thinking, in which there is normal and abnormal, adequate or deficient, and a move toward seeing the brain as having many, many differences which may result in atypical behavior or development for some, but which may not necessarily be related to ability or intellect. This is also a move away from evaluating behavior with ability.

For example, neuroscientists, with brain imaging technology, can now identify areas of the brain that are structurally different in people who have ADHD, as well as other neurological differences. They also know that those with ADHD may lag a bit behind the general population in reaching neurological maturity. Thus, interventions or strategies in education that respond to this condition could very well greatly increase the success of those with ADHD in their academic endeavors. The brain is plastic. It can and does change in response to experience.

The differences found in those who have ADHD have almost nothing to do with intelligence and almost everything to do with developmental stage. This is but one example. Even in the neurotypical population there are wide ranges of difference. For example, boys and girls have different rates and sequences of neurological development. Girls who read at grade level in first grade are "normal." Boys who do not read at grade level are "below average." In reality, both are on track. Girls' verbal skills develop sooner than those of boys, and it is disadvantageous to boys to evaluate their reading skills at age six by the same criteria as those for girls.

As scientists have increasingly come to understand, there is no such thing as a "normal" brain. It is as foolish to say there is a normal brain as to assert that there is a normal nose or eyebrow. There are typical features, but no nose or eyebrow is identical to any other. Even on the same face, these features are likely to be asymmetrical. Our brains are no different. Indeed, it is less likely for the brain to be similar to others because it is a dynamic, changing, adaptive organ. For educators, understanding the neurological uniqueness of each learner is one of the key requirements for effective education in the 21st century.

Difference, Not Disease

"The Truth About Autism: Scientists Reconsider What they Think they Know," presents a startlingly different picture of autism than the one that is typically offered. This is the title of an article that appeared in the February, 2008 issue of *Wired* magazine. The subject of the article, Amanda Baggs, is 27 years old, autistic, and non-verbal. She also has created and manages a blog about autism which to date has had more than 300,000 hits, leading to interviews by the media and to invitations to visit scientists who study autism.

Although she cannot speak, she can type, and enters her thoughts into a computer that translates her typed words to speech. She is creative, intelligent, and articulate. Such innovations have been able to expose the fallacy of a condition that has been thought of as being trapped "in the solitary isolation of the mind." Today, many neuroscientists are abandoning the idea that autism is a disease that can be "cured."

Rather, they are replacing the disease model with a "difference model." Albeit that some 75 percent of those with autism are diagnosed as being mentally retarded, it is very likely that the measures we use are simply inappropriate for the autistic brain, and this is a central concept in the difference model of autism which holds that we should not think of the autistic brain, which includes Asperger's Syndrome, as defective, but rather as different.

Thomas Zeffiro, a Massachusetts General Hospital neuroscientist and one of the leading proponents of the difference model noted in the *Wired* article that "If Amanda Baggs had walked into my clinic five years ago, I would have said she was a low-functioning autistic with significant cognitive impairment. And I would have been totally wrong."

Helping Students with Asperger's

Keep in mind that Asperger's Syndrome is a disorder on the autism continuum. Some students are more severely impaired than others. Not every student with Asperger's responds the same way in a given situation. There are some broad behavioral similarities, but students with Asperger's are as individual as any others. This makes it even more difficult to understand. It would be so easy if educators could know that there were predictable, known responses to certain situations. But there are not.

The following suggestions are ways to help you work effectively with students who have autism disorders. These strategies will allow you to get to know the Asperger's student and to be more successful in developing educational strategies that will work.

1. Don't ask broad, open-ended questions.

Don't ask broad, open-ended questions such as "what can I do to help," or "what do you want me to do" when meeting with a student having academic struggles or other problems. Most students with

Asperger's Syndrome or other HFA (high-functioning autism) will not be able to answer these questions very well. If a student is having a problem, remember that he or she may see the world in a very concrete, black and white way. If an assignment is due on Tuesday, and the student has been unable to complete it, asking "What do you want me to do?" is not a good question. The student may believe that there are no alternatives, and thus, nothing that you can do to help.

2. Look for facts, not feelings.

Instead of open-ended, broad questions, or questions that ask for the student to tell you how he or she feels about something, ask very concrete, probing questions that will allow the student to give specific, factual answers. Guide the student into explaining what is going on in a particular class or in general in school that is affecting his or her performance. This will help you to develop an understanding of the issues, and help the student structure a strategy. For example:

What makes this class hard for you? What would make this class easier for you? What makes it hard for you to meet the deadlines? What gives you the most trouble in this class? Do you have this problem in other classes or with other teachers? What is different in this class that causes the problem? Are there things that confuse you in this class? Why is this confusing? What is different in other classes that keeps you from being as confused? What could be done in this class that would make it work better for you?

Build a picture of the student's experience. By asking these types of questions, you can begin to build a picture of the student's experience. Once you have this, you can summarize what you understand. Ask the student frequently if your understandings are correct. They may not be, because often precise communication is very difficult for students with Asperger's and HFA. This kind of dialog will also help you build trust with the student, which is especially important with students who have autism disorders. Often they have not had good experiences in interacting with adults and authority figures.

Begin to explore concrete specific action solutions. Once you and the student have agreed upon the issues that are creating problems for the student, you can begin to explore solutions. Solutions will likely involve things the student can do (very concrete, specific actions) and/ or things the teacher might do differently to help resolve difficulties.

For example, a daily e-mail from the student to the teacher summarizing understandings of assignments might be something the student could do to make sure he or she is on track. Being flexible with deadlines if the student is struggling with an assignment might be something the teacher can do. The responsibility for success of the student with an autism disorder is a shared one. Both the student and teacher may need to alter their normal ways of doing things. The absolute most important thing for the teacher to do is to be non-judgmental, supportive, and helpful with suggesting viable solutions to problems. Once a strategy has been devised, the teacher should not assume that everything is on track. The student may not be able to pursue the strategy without more discussion as he or she begins to work on things. If the student knows that he or she can come back to the teacher again for more clarification, without having to worry about being scolded, this will greatly enhance the student's ability to develop responsibility for his or her work and to be academically successful.

A positive relationship between the student and teacher is essential, and it is important for the student to feel he or she can bring concerns to the teacher without risk of being criticized or being told that there is no flexibility in procedures. It is unlikely that most students with autism disorders who are high functioning will be manipulative in such situations. Being manipulative, lying to gain advantage, and knowingly breaking rules are behaviors that are very difficult for most people with autism disorders to carry out. Most operate by a very strict moral code and tend to follow rules as they understand them. If there appears to be manipulation, discuss this in a non-judgmental way with the student. It may be that you will get a better understanding of what is going on with the student. If there really is manipulation going on, then you can address it specifically.

Clear understandings and expectations key to success. Clear strategies, clear expectations, clear understandings, are the keys to success for the student with an autism disorder. It is possible to know whether the student's understandings are clear only if you ask him or her. Thus, when the student does not turn in an assignment, does not "answer the question" posed for an essay, or says he/she didn't know that an assignment was due, it is always important to ask why.

3. Suspend Disbelief.

One of the most challenging demands of working with a student with an autism disorder is to set aside all assumptions about what may be motivating your student, causing him or her to have problems or not to meet expectations. There is only one assumption that should be made, and that is that the student wants to succeed and wants to do well, wants to meet expectations. By talking with the student, you can see how he or she is undertaking to meet the requirements. It may not be a successful strategy, and it may not appear that the student is putting in his or her best effort. Remember that the student with an autism disorder generally has a very literal (black and white) view of things; thus if they tell you what they understood to be expected, and it is wrong, it nevertheless most likely reflects their perception.

4. Listen, listen, listen.

It is extremely important to listen carefully, to avoid contradicting the student or challenging his or her explanation. The student may not have seen things correctly, but this is the nature of autism. By listening, you can better understand the process of logic that the student used in order to determine how to complete the assigned work. The only way a teacher can really understand and appropriately evaluate the work of a student with autism disorder is to try to understand what the student believed expectations to be. Once you have an idea of what works and does not work for the student and your ideas are confirmed by the student, begin to develop strategies. Be careful to do this slowly and in a measured way. Students with autism disorders may be overwhelmed if too many ideas are put on the table at one time.

Do not expect the student to propose options. Do not expect the student to propose options - at least not at first. He or she might, but this is not necessarily likely. If a student does propose an option, do not dismiss it out of hand, even if it is a poor idea.

Discuss the pros and cons. Discuss the pros and cons, and if it is not viable, discuss why. Here is an example:

Student proposal: I don't want to go to my first block class. I haven't done all the assignments and my teacher will be "all over" me about that, or she will want to talk to me about it, and I don't know what to say.

Since simply not going to class is a poor option, it needs to be discussed. Don't say, "Well, you have to go to class. That is just a requirement." Instead, try some of the following responses:

"I can see why you don't want to go to that class. Let's look at some things that might make going less stressful. What do you think would help?"

The student may then say, "I don't know." Not because he or she doesn't have an idea, but because he or she may feel that there is no acceptable answer. Should this happen, try something like, "Well, let's look at some things you can do so that you feel more comfortable. I know you don't feel ready to talk with your teacher about this, but you need to go to class. Here are two things you might consider:

- Go to your teacher at the beginning of the class and tell her that you know you need to talk over some things, but that you don't feel ready to do that. Tell her that you want to talk with your counselor/advisor/etc. first. Then, tell her you will make an appointment with her, and do it.
- Go to class, and if your teacher says she needs to talk with you, tell her you need to talk with her as well, but that you need to consult with your advisor first. Then tell her you will set up a time, and do it.

The key here is to give the student some strategies for handling the expected response of his teacher and to help minimize stress. Concrete suggestions about appropriate behavior and potential responses to what he or she fears encountering can help the student be more successful. This is not unlike role play, which is a very successful teaching tool for students with autism disorders. If the student feels prepared for what he or she might encounter, then the stress of going to class will be reduced. Be sure to have the student repeat back to you what the options are for handling the situation. If he or she cannot do that, it means that your suggestions will not be helpful and most likely that the student has not understood how to apply them.

5. Plan Strategically.

If a student with an autism disorder is performing poorly, particularly if that student has demonstrated competence in the past, it is very important not to make assumptions about why the student's performance is slipping, but rather to talk with the student about what has changed in the school environment or circumstance that has caused the problem. Once this has been worked out, through careful dialog, you can help the student develop strategies for improving his or her situation.

It may be helpful for you to outline scenarios. With each scenario, it is important to be very specific and clear about all requirements and considerations for each scenario. Do not develop more than a couple (three maximum) of options with the student. It may be too confusing to process a large amount of information. You might ask the student to summarize any options that you develop, and make sure that each option is outlined in written form for the student to review.

You may want a follow-up discussion. You may want a follow-up discussion with the student in order to make a final decision on how to proceed, which option is best, etc. The student may need some time to reflect upon and process the information. In the follow-up discussion, you may even find that the student's understanding is quite different from what you thought it was, now that the information has been processed. If this happens, you have another opportunity to clarify.

6. Avoid being judgmental.

Avoid being judgmental. Always keep in mind that a student with Asperger's or HFA may not respond to comments, observations or direction in the same way that other students might.

Do not tell them to take responsibility. Avoid telling students that they "need to take responsibility" for themselves, or that they "need to apply themselves," and things of this nature. They most likely already know this. These concepts are broad and abstract, and may have little meaning unless concrete ways of demonstrating the behaviors are discussed.

They may already be applying themselves. In all likelihood, they may already be applying themselves to the greatest extent possible and they may be taking responsibility for themselves as fully as they know how. Their efforts simply may not be meeting with success. Their way of "taking responsibility" just may not look like the way you would do it or the way other students would do it, or the way you think a student should be behaving to demonstrate responsibility and effort.

You should ask the student about it. It could be very instructional and help you to understand that the typical strategies of "working harder," "coming in early to discuss the problem," etc., may not only not work for the student, but may actually make things worse. It can also help you understand the strategies that the student is using and help you know what does work for that student.

Taking responsibility is different. For a student with Asperger's syndrome, "taking responsibility" may look very different from the normal expectation. For such a student, it is important to avoid becoming overwhelmed, because this leads to dysfunctional behavior. By the time they are in high school, most students with Asperger's syndrome know when life is becoming overwhelming and when they need to limit the demands being made on them. Managing input and meeting demands have to be very carefully controlled, and often, for students with HFA or Aspergers, taking responsibility means limiting the amount of stimulation and demand, not increasing it. It means taking frequent breaks and taking lots of down time. One thing at a time. If a student notes that he or she does better when focusing on one thing at a time, it is important to understand that this may mean "to the complete exclusion of everything else." Thus, if a student is focusing on English, it may mean that assignments and deadlines are missed in social studies and science, for example. It is critical for teachers to understand that this does not represent a cavalier attitude about work, but rather, just the opposite. It is a strategy, which, if allowed, will make it possible for the student to manage multiple demands in a measured way, and which will prevent the student from becoming overwhelmed and dysfunctional. When the English requirement is met, the student can then turn to science or social studies.

7. Help the student repeat success.

Don't assume that if a student handles a situation well one time, he or she will necessarily be able to do it again. Often students with HFA and Asperger's Syndrome do not generalize their learning from one situation to another. The learning experience may need to be repeated several times before the student will be able to apply the lessons he/she is learning about how to effectively handle situations related to academic performance.

8. Eliminate additional external pressures.

Recognize that students with Asperger's Syndrome who have shown effort and high achievement are probably putting a lot of pressure on themselves to succeed. Realize that in order to be successful, they must work enormously hard - harder than many other students who achieve at their level. Additional external pressures to improve performance may be very counterproductive and do more harm than good. The need is for support and guidance, not necessarily direction and motivation. Educators need to listen to the student carefully. Accept his or her explanations as being reflective of his or her understandings, whether those understandings are accurate or not. Recognize that it is possible that teachers or others may have felt they were being very specific about requirements and expectations, but that the student may truly not have understood clearly. This is a no fault situation. There is no blame to be placed, either on the teacher for being unclear or on the student for failing to understand. The only problems arise if the student is assumed to be inattentive, unmotivated, lacking in focus - responsible for the problem.

9. Understand that they do not lie.

Realize that it is common for students with Asperger's Syndrome, because of their very literal view of the world, to be almost unable to be dishonest, tell a lie, or be manipulative. Always give the benefit of the doubt to the student.

10. Ask the student to explain it.

When you have discussed a strategy or understanding with the student, don't ask if he/she understands it. The student may believe that it is understood when it is not. Ask the student to explain his or her understanding. That will give you an opportunity to correct any misconceptions that may have been communicated.

11. You need to set up meetings.

Realize that you will probably need to be pro-active with students in setting up meetings, discussions of work, and addressing problems. While the student may know there is a problem, he or she may believe nothing can be done (there are rules, and students with Asperger's often do not consider that anything outside the stated procedures can be possible), may not know what to ask, what can be asked, or how to ask for help.

Unfortunately, most Asperger's students have had ample experience with adults who are judgmental rather than helpful or who simply reinforce that the responsibility lies with the student, who already knows that but doesn't know what to do differently. So the student may not see how it is in their best interest to approach the teacher or staff person. When teachers wait for the student who is struggling to initiate communication, then the situation grows worse - for everyone. The student may be seen as not being concerned enough to seek assistance, an inaccurate perception, and the overall situation continues to deteriorate, grades continue to suffer and stress continues to increase.

12. Counselors should repeat information.

Adult counselors need to make sure that this information is clear, and again, that it is repeated over and over again. Just saying, "my door is always open," or "he/she knows they can always come and talk to me," or "I'm here a half hour before class starts every day," may all be things the student knows, but which are not adequate to assure that the student will be able to take advantage of the resources.

Communicating with Asperger's and Autism Students

Realize that students may respond to some questions in ways that are inaccurate, but not intentionally dishonest. Here are some reasons why:

- They may be overwhelmed and just want to reduce their stress, so they may say what they think the teacher wants to hear.
- They may be so overwhelmed that they don't really know what is being asked, so they say what they think needs to be said.
- When there is too much stimulation in the environment, too much stress, or too much environmental "noise," a student with an autism disorder may simply "shut down." He or she may seem unresponsive and disengaged. He or she may answer "I don't know" to simple questions, such as "why didn't you turn in this assignment." This is no more controllable for the student with autism than seizures are for the student with epilepsy. It is harder to understand, because it is not so dramatic, but it is not dissimilar. In both situations, a neurological signal is being sent - a signal over which the individual has no control.
- They may misunderstand, at a very basic level, what is being asked. The answer they give may be to the question as they understand it, but not at the teacher intends it.

Here is an example of how subtlety in language can lead to confusion. A teacher assigned students a project of keeping a notebook related to class activities. At the end of the quarter, the teacher told the students to turn in their notes. All the students in the class, except the student with Asperger's syndrome, turned in their notebooks. That student tore out the notes and turned them in, raising the ire of the teacher who considered that to be oppositional behavior. The student explained that he was not asked to turn in his notebook. He was asked to turn in his notes.

Another example is of a student who is not focusing on an in-class assignment. The teacher tells the student that if he doesn't want to do the assignment, he can just "go to the office." The student, not recognizing that this was a way of telling him that he would be disciplined if he did not do the assignment just got up and went to the office – something he preferred over doing the assignment. The literal way in which Asperger's students understand language can create lots of misunderstanding.

No Fault Pedagogy

Don't assume that because you have a plan for solving a specific problem, it is necessarily going to work. For example, students may be given extended time on a test, but if the setting they must use for the test-taking is not quiet enough, or private enough, or is physically cluttered or is in some other way uncomfortable for the student, the extended time option may not help at all.

It is extremely difficult for teachers and staff to understand when a student with autism withdraws or pulls back from interaction. It is seen, usually, as a flaw in the individual student, as a sign of lack of motivation, of laziness, or of "just not caring." The responsibility, for teachers in schools that choose to admit students with autism disorders, is to understand that they must deal with these students somewhat differently from other students.

There is nothing, ever, that teachers can do to make the student with an autism disorder think, behave, or act like a student who is not autistic. This is not to say that the student cannot perform brilliantly in an academic setting, but the student may need to take a different path to demonstrate his/her abilities or may need more support and direction to learn how to perform well. Indeed, it is well documented that many people with autism disorders are extremely intellectually capable, even gifted.

To nurture this ability, it is essential for effectively teaching the autistic person, to allow the student to demonstrate his or her academic competence in ways that give an accurate picture of ability. While this will usually be no different from the ways in which others are evaluated, there may be times when the autistic student's work needs to be considered differently. Maybe a presentation needs to be accepted as a written assignment rather than a verbal one, for example. Maybe there needs to be modification of homework assignments, as long as the student demonstrates mastery in the final evaluation. Maybe the student needs extra time to do an assignment, and deadlines need to be extended.

Autism is not "curable"

It is not possible to learn one's way out of autism. It is possible only to learn how to cope with it, how to manage it, and how to develop strategies that help minimize performance in areas of deficit, and this requires the understanding, flexibility, patience, and realization on the part of educators that every student is an individual; that to adequately teach and educate students with autism disorders, this individuality must be respected; strategies must be put in place to respond to it, and these strategies may be quite different from those that work for students who are not autistic - they may even fly in the face of accepted pedagogy.

Effectively teaching a student who has an autism disorder also means going beyond lip service in treating students as individuals. It means being flexible. It means developing a dialog with the student and listening to him or her and working with him or her in a very specific and intentional way to help the student grow and improve his or her skills. It means letting the students tell you what they need, and it means that helping them to do this if they can't manage it alone - until they can do it on their own. It means understanding that if a student appears unresponsive, the lack of affect that characterizes Asperger's syndrome makes that quite predictable. The behavior, body language and interaction from the student may not represent, at all, what he or she is feeling or thinking. Ultimately, these students will be able to manage independently, but it may take them longer than it takes other students to learn the necessary skills.

Effective teaching of students with autism disorders

Effective teaching of students with autism disorders means responding positively to what they say, not challenging it or doubting it or dismissing it because it seems inaccurate to you. It means probing, questioning, seeking understanding, asking for clarification, re-stating and clarifying, over and over again.

It means understanding that what you have done as a teacher or administrator may not get the desired result, even when you did your best, did what you thought needed to be done, what you thought would work for the student - and that if it doesn't work, it is not your fault.

It also means understanding that if it does not work, it is not the student's fault, either. It means not assuming that since you did what you should have done, any problem is the result of a student who is not doing his or her best. For students with autism disorders who are generally high achievers, this is rarely the case. It simply means that it is time to back up and start over with more clarity. It means initiating a conversation with your student to find out why things didn't work as they should have. It means letting the student tell you why things didn't go as well as they might have. This will benefit both of you. It means recognizing that you may need to do things differently if you are going to be a good teacher or counselor for a student with an autism disorder. It means working hard.

It also means, in the last analysis, that if you do not do these things and your student fails, the failure is also shared.

Students with Asperger's and autism have a gift. It is as much a strength as it is a weaknesses. There are already companies that will not hire "normal" people and only hire people with autism, because autistic workers have superior spatial and math skills that enable them to work more productively and profitably. Students with Asperger's and autism give us as educators a wonderful place to begin seeing learners not as having disabilities, but as having strengths, weaknesses, and different learning styles.

In summary, maximizing the learning experience and success of a student with Asperger's and autism not only benefits that person, but society where each and every knowledge worker is a valuable contributor. Finding those strengths, that gift, and fostering it is a rewarding educational adventure. For society it has literally golden results; for you as educator it also provides satisfaction for a job well taught.

Conclusion

This is an exciting time to be teaching or otherwise involved with education. What is emerging is a new model for the school and college of the 21st century that will be superior to the factory model of the last century. As education becomes personalised and customized to each student, schools and colleges will be able to maximize the skills and strengths of each student, giving each student his or her best shot at a prosperous and intellectually fulfilling life. Education will be better, and life will be better for our students and our grandchildren, the goal of every parent and every teacher.

Along the way you have the opportunity to observe with fascination how our young people adapt to the new reality of the Internet Age. We also have a window of opportunity to look back at how our elders addressed the same transition 100 years ago as society and education moved from the Agrarian Age into the Industrial Age.

At the same time as we look to the very old for guidance and watch the very young as they create this new age, we also have the chance to be "players" in creating the new educational system of the 21st century. You can explore, test and try innovative techniques and strategies. You can join the discussion on how education should look.

Education is now more critical to the success of our society than ever before, and your role and contributions more welcome than ever.

This is a great time to be an educator, to be both a learner in the new century, and to share your wisdom and knowledge. Have a great 21st century.

Appendix A.
Pedagogy Predictions for 2030

1. The way most teachers grade today will be declared illegal. Grading based on behavior, including penalizing students for lack of attendance, handing in homework late, and not doing course assignments, will be illegal.

2. A significant part of education funding will come from a tax on marijuana sales and usage.

3. Boys will again be 50% of college entrants and graduates.

4. The United States, joining other post-industrial nations, will declare that 50% or more of its children should have four-year college degrees, thus doubling the number of students in college over the number in 2010.

5. Technology budgets will be larger than building or capital improvement budgets.

6. Almost all teachers will not be allowed to grade students. Grading will be done by specialists, who will administer and evaluate tests.

7. The Carnegie Unit and Student Hour will be replaced by an outcomes-based learning measurement.

8. Students will take tests, on average, once or twice a week, almost always online.

9. The A, B, C, D, F system of grading will be replaced by pass-fail tests, with 80% being the pass rate.

10. Students in elementary, secondary and higher education will be allowed to choose from around 10,000 subjects to study.

11. Schools and colleges will have classes 18 hours a day.

12. Students will not attend school or college continually from morning to mid-afternoon, but instead study at home, school and in the community, often on the same day.

13. Elementary and secondary students will travel up to 100 miles each way to school each day, taking trains.

14. While 55% of students took school buses to schools in 2009, only about 20% or fewer will take school buses by 2030. Some 80% of students will walk and/or take light rail or trains.

15. Community colleges and public university systems will consolidate a number of operations and use a multi-campus approach where students travel by train between campuses.

16. Most schools will offer online courses as part of elementary and secondary education.

17. Every face-to-face course in elementary, secondary and post-secondary education will be hybrid.

18. Testing, which will occur at least weekly for each student, will be done by objective independent sources trained and skilled in testing and assessment.

19. The physical classroom with a blackboard, teacher in front, and rows of desks will all be gone from most schools and colleges, replaced by one or more versions of a "learning commons."

20. Governments, schools and colleges all endorse a policy that personalises learning and instruction, abandoning the factory model of education.

21. Faculty and administrators will cease treating, and saying that they treat, students the "same," and treat, and say they treat, each student "differently."

Appendix B.
45 Tips for Teachers to Do Now

Technology
1. All assignments should be posted online.
2. All scores and grades should be posted online.
3. Use your students as techies.
4. Encourage students to learn online.
5. Have a virtual team project.
6. Have some multimedia student presentations.
7. Find your passion, engage in one technology.
8. Move your classroom to hybrid.

Helping Gen Y learn
9. Incorporate multimedia into your teaching.
10. Do some collaborative projects.
11. Encourage students to teach each other.
12. Encourage students to create content.
13. Give online work assignments.
14. Provide very specific instructions for assignments.
15. Post all lectures online, reduce or eliminate in-person lectures.

Helping girls learn more
16. Revise homework and coursework to pass/fail to devalue the perfection of an 'A.'
17. Challenge female students to spend less time per module, and to tackle more challenging modules.
18. Reward passing harder tests more than getting 'A's on easier work.
19. Do not reward behavior (turning work in on time, for example).

20. Reward failure, especially on new challenges.

Helping boys succeed
21. Teach boys how to fidget; do not discourage them from fidgeting.
22. Sit next to a male when helping him, not across.
23. Have more frequent physical activity, such as allowing students to stand.
24. Visualize and treat boys as being 2 years younger than they actually are.
25. Create abstract problem-solving and moral debates.
26. Give them new challenges.
27. Look at boys' test scores, not homework, to tell how much they are learning.
28. Speak more loudly so boys can hear you better.

Both boys and girls
29. Provide extended time for those who need it.
30. Offer alternative exercises and ways of learning.
31. Expect high-level performance, but do not equate that with work.
32. Never write with cursive.
33. Be wrong. Say "I don't know" whenever it is true
34. Do not punish, do not be negative, do not threaten
35. Encourage them to create content

Grading
36. Maximize each student's testing environment.
37. Allow, encourage and reward re-do and failure.
38. Allow 'quiz outs' of homework.
39. Use multiple assessments and frequent testing.
40. Do not grade based on behavior. No penalty for lack of attendance, late work, or "not doing the work."
41. Move towards learning contracts (IEPs).

For Yourself
42. Make your own Action Plan
43. Do 1-3 21st century things
44. Fail. Be a pioneer.
45. Have a great time learning from the kids!

References

Introduction: Welcome to the 21st Century

1. For more on how learning is changing, see *Generational Learning Styles* by Julie Coates, Learning Resources Network, River Falls, Wisconsin, 2007.

2. For example, to understand the rationale behind online learning, see *Advanced Teaching Online* by William A. Draves, Learning Resources Network, River Falls, Wisconsin, 2000, 2001 and 2007 (Third Edition).

3. *Nine Shift: Work,life and education in the 21st Century* by William A. Draves and Julie Coates, Learning Resources Network, River Falls, Wisconsin, 2004.

4. The term "andragogy" was first introduced in education by Malcolm Knowles, the father of modern adult education, and author of numerous books on adult learning.

Chapter 1.
Nine Shift: Work, life and education in the 21st century

1. The transformation from the Agrarian Age to the Industrial Age was chronicled in many of the last century's top novels. The first arguably to do so was *Main Street,* by Sinclair Lewis, Harcourt Brace Jovanovich, Inc., New York, 1920.

2. See the *Statistical History of the U.S.,* Fairfield Publishers, page 74; And *Statistical Abstract of the U.S.,* National Data Book, 1996, page 410.

3. *Managing in the Next Society,* by Peter F. Drucker, Truman Talley Books, New York, 2002, pages 129, 296 and 299. It is interesting to note that Frederick Allen, writing about the changes 100 years ago in The Big Change, acknowledges the work of Peter Drucker in summarizing proceedings from a conference in 1951 that led to Allen's undertaking of his history.

4. *The Essential Drucker,* by Peter F. Drucker, Harper Collins Publishers, New York, NY, 2001, pages 304-305.

5. *The Big Change,* by Frederick Lewis Allen, Harper & Brothers, New York, 1952.

6. Kathleen McMonigal, University of Washington, Seattle, speech before the 17th Annual Distance Teaching and Learning Conference, Madison, Wisconsin, 2001.

7. "Telecommuting will become a mainstay in Corporate America," says a story on *MSNBC,* reporting on a Gartner Dataquest report (April 2007) on the rise of telecommuters from around 10% of workers to close to 30% of employees telecommuting part or full time. See "Telecommuting: The Quiet Revolution," by Eve Tahmincioglu, October 5, 2007, http://www.msnbc.msn.com/id/20281475/.

8. Net Gain, by John Hagel III and Arthur G. Armstrong, Harvard Business School Press, Boston, MA, 1996. A seminal work in understanding networks and the changing economics brought about by the Internet.

9. *The Centerless Corporation,* by Bruce A. Pasternack and Albert J. Viscio, Simon & Schuster, New York, NY, 1998, a pioneering work on understanding business units and the network structure.

10. Draves has been documenting Generation Y's switch from cars to trains. Evidence includes record train ridership since 2005, rise in car sharing, opinion surveys by Pew Research, and the decline in regis-

tered drivers among the young. In 2010 Draves discovered data in The National Household Transportation Survey, Federal Highway Administration, Department of Transportation, which showed that young people were driving 37% less in 2009 than young people did in 1995, as a percentage of total miles driven. He also found that while people over 40 were just 46% of the population, they drove 59% of the miles. DOT data also shows that driving declines after age 65, meaning that by 2020 a majority of Boomers will be over age 65, contributing to the decline in driving. He was interviewed by *Advertising Age*, "Is Digital Revolution Driving Decline in U.S. Car Culture?" by Jack Neff, Editor at Large, *Advertising Age*, May 31, 2010.

The percentage of young people who say an auto is a necessity has plunged in the last 3 years, according to a Pew Research Center study. Dr. Wendy Wang, lead researcher for the study, provided us with the data. In April 2009 some 93% of people aged 50-64 said the auto was a necessity. However, only 80% of people aged 18-29 said the auto was a necessity. In 2006, the different generations both agreed the auto was a necessity, both coming in at 92%. The huge decline in Gen Y's attitude caused the whole population's rating of the auto as a necessity to decline 3 points, down to 88% overall. http://pewresearch. org/pubs/1199/more-items-seen-as-luxury-not-necessity?src=prc-latest&proj=peoplepress

11. "Wrong Turn," by Malcolm Gladwell, *The New Yorker*, June 11, 2001, page 55.

12. The World Health Organization puts automobile accidents as the third most preventable cause of death in the world. More than one million people die from automobile accidents every year.

13. Cities grew 0.97% in 2008, up from 0.90% two years ago and up big time from around 0.5% some 4-7 years ago. Suburbs grew 1.11%, but that is down big time from 1.48% some 4-7 years ago. So the trend (cities grow faster, suburbs grow more slowly and then start to decline) started around 2002. See "Cities Grow at Suburbs' Expense," *The Wall Street Journal*, July 1, 2009. Neff, in *Advertising Age*, also cites data showing the biggest return in housing prices in 2010 were in neighborhoods located near train and light rail stations.

Chapter 2.
The Mission of Education: Only One Thing Matters

1. "Teaching young people is not the primary objective anymore, and that's wrong," says Claudia Dreifus, co-author with Andrew Hacker of *Higher Education?*, Holt/Times Books, New York, 2010.

2. "The U.S., once the world's leader in the percentage of young people with college degrees, has fallen to 12th among 36 developed nations. According to a news report from the College Board, the U.S. is 12th among developed nations in the percentage of 25 to 34-year olds with college degrees. 'While the nation struggles to strengthen the economy,' the report said, 'the educational capacity of our country continues to decline.'" "Putting Our Brains On Hold," by Bob Herbert, *The New York Times,* August 6, 2010.

3. "Increasing so-called human capital levels is widely seen as critical to prosperity in a knowledge-based economy. Skilled employees tend to make each other more productive, and large concentrations of them in a metropolitan area boost not only the average income but the wages of less-educated workers, some researchers have found." "Price tag for UW plan to issue more degrees: $22.6 million," by Sharif Durhams and Rick Romell, *The Milwaukee Journal Sentinel,* August 16, 2010.

Chapter 3.
Curriculum in the 21st Century: Does content matter?

1. "How will flexible curriculum work?" *BBC online,* February 5, 2007, http://news.bbc.co.uk/2/hi/uk_news/education/6332537.stm.

2. "Drucker on Schools," by Harold Jarche, October 31, 2004, http://www.jarche.com/2004/10/OLD349/.

3. "No Subjects, No teachers, No Schools, No Peers – Just problems: Arguments for a minimalist approach for maximising the scope of problem-based learning," Tan and Lim Ai Ming, 2005. http://pbl.tp.edu.sg/Understanding PBL/Articles/TamLim(no-Subj).pdf

4. "Teachers' Roles in Teaching and Problem Solving," by Harold Jarche, November 15, 2005, http://www.jarche.com/2005/11/old641/.

5. "Curriculum for 'changing society'," *BBC online*, February 5, 2007, http://news.bbc.co.uk/2/hi/uk_news/education/6330961.stm

6. "Grace Dunham still remembers a typical sixth-grade day at St. Ann's School (Brooklyn, New York): She played guitar, made papier-mache aliens for Jupiter's moon Europa, dropped an egg off a balcony for a project that involved creating protective covers to prevent eggs from breaking. Ms. Dunham, now 18, has just graduated from St. Ann's, the private school in Brooklyn (New York) Heights that has no grades, few rules and exceptionally good admissions to some of the country's most elite colleges. Ms. Dunham is headed to Brown University." From "A Leader's Record at a Brooklyn school," by Jenny Anderson, *The New York Times*, July 20, 2010.

7. *Experience & Education,* by John Dewey, Simon & Schuster, New York, 1938, page 67.

8. For more on designing a learner plan, and guidelines for contract learning, see *Self-Directed Learning: A guide for learners and teachers,* by Malcolm Knowles, Association Press, Follett Publishing Company, Chicago, 1975.

9. See also "Harnessing Technology: Transforming Learning and Children's Services," Department for Education and Skills, United Kingdom, DFES-1296-2005, March 2005.

Chapter 4.
From Pedagogy to Andragogy: The New Role for Teachers

1. The impact of teacher quality has been verified by almost every education study. One illustration is a study by Raj Chetty, a Harvard economist, who found that children with a high class test performance in kindergarten made more money in their twenties, as well as being more likely to go to college and save for retirement, than children with lower test performance scores in kindergarten. See "The Case for $320,000 Kindergarten Teachers," by David Leonhardt, *The New York Times,* July 28, 2010.   201

Eric Hanushek, an economist at Stanford, estimates that the students of a very bad teacher will learn, on average, half a year's worth of material in one school year. The students in the class of a very good teacher will learn a year and a half's worth of material. That difference amounts to a year's worth of learning in a single year. Teacher effects dwarf school effects: your child is actually better off in a "bad" school with an excellent teacher than in an excellent school with a bad teacher. From "Most Likely to Succeed," by Malcolm Gladwell, *The New Yorker,* December 15, 2008. http://www.newyorker.com/reporting/2008/12/15/081215fa_fact_gladwell?currentPage=all

2. *The Adult Learner,* the definitive classic in adult education and human resource development, by Malcolm Knowles, Fifth Edition, Gulf Publishing Company, Houston, Texas, 1998.

3. For example a British study reported by the BBC concluded, "There is no evidence that children in smaller primary classes do better in math or English, researchers say." This from "The effect of class size on attainment and classroom processes in English primary schools (Years 4 to 6) 2000-2003" by Peter Blatchford, Paul Bassett, Penelope Brown, Clare Martin and Anthony Russell, Institute of Education, University of London. See "Small class pupils do no better," *BBC Online,* January 5, 2005, http://news.bbc.co.uk/2/hi/uk_news/education/4146977.stm

"A bad teacher with thirty kids will be a bad teacher with thirteen kids," says Ron Clark, 2000 Disney Teacher of the Year, who has taught in Harlem and in schools in other low income communities. He says class size has no relevance to student achievement. Source: Ron Clark, keynote address, Institute for Credentialing Excellence, Atlanta, November 17, 2010.

4. Certified Online Instructor (COI) is a voluntary certification for online teachers, primarily online faculty in higher education. It is administered and taught by online experts, chaired by Dr. Mary Dereshiwsky of Northern Arizona University, working with the Learning Resources Network (LERN), the largest association in continuing education in the world. The authors teach and work with the COI program. For more, see http://www.teachingonthenet.org/courses/certified_online_instructor/index.cfm.

5. For example, weekly math quizzes used to take 5 to 15 minutes of classroom time for one K-12 teacher. He reported that just putting weekly math quizzes online added two weeks of instructional time per semester to each of his classes. Reported by Connie Jaeger, Computer Science Chair, Homestead High School, Mequon-Thienesville, Wisconsin, and Victoria Lovejoy, Department Chair of Sciences, Rolling Hills Prep School, San Pedro, California, in "Implementing and supporting hybrid online learning in a K-12 environment" session at the 26th Annual Conference on Distance Teaching & Learning, Madison, Wisconsin, August 5, 2010.

6. Teachers and faculty are creating an increasing number of techniques and strategies to not only conserve teacher time but also to enhance student learning. One way for students to engage in collaborative learning is to have students in one group in the class take notes during the class and post them for the entire class online, thus freeing up the other students to listen and not have to take notes at the same time.

Another way to save teacher time is to have the teacher post class notes online before the class occurs. In a third example, one instructor insists that students ask three other classmates his or her question before coming to the teacher for the answer. These tips reported by Jaeger and Lovejoy.

7. Data analysis has enormous implications for education and learning, as in other fields. For example, in 2010 scientists were able to greatly enhance their ability to predict at what age a person might get Alzheimer's. The increased predictive ability was not the result of any discovery, but simply by being able to gather databases and analyze more data. See "Making Strides to Predict Alzheimer's," Stephanie Lederman, Executive Director, American Federation of Aging Research, *The New York Times,* August 11, 2010.

Chapter 5.
Learning and Teaching: The 21 Pedagogical Concepts

1. Richard Thieme, keynote, Lifelong Learning Annual Conference, Chicago, November 21, 2000.

2. Laura Taylor interview with Julie Coates, Raleigh, NC, November 2005.

3. See *Advanced Teaching Online,* by William A. Draves.

Gareth Mitchell, one of the world's foremost technology reporters and host of the weekly radio program "Digital Planet" on the BBC, reports that in the Netherlands students are encouraged to keep their cell phones on in school, as cell phones represent an excellent way to access the web and information for their studies. Source: Technology discussion with Gareth Mitchell, November 7, 2010, Chicago, at the annual conference of the Learning Resources Network (LERN). Julie contrasts this embracing of technology in education with a general fear or hesitancy about educational technology in the United States, where cell phones are required to be off during school hours.

4. The original work on the "no significant difference" evidence between online courses and face-to-face courses was done by educators at the University of Alberta. Another source is http://www.nosignificantdifference.org

In 2009 *Education Week* published the story suggesting that online learning might be starting to be better than purely in-person classes. See "Research Shows Evolving Picture of E-Education, by Debra Viadero, at http://www.edweek.org/ew/articles/2009/03/26/26research.h28.html

Two of the first articles to suggest that online courses were superior to in-person only courses were:

"UWM online psych students outperform those in lecture hall class," by Erica Perez, *Milwaukee Journal-Sentinel,* February 1, 2009; and

"Study Finds That Online Education Beats the Classroom," by Steve Lohr, *The New York Times* Blog, August 18, 2009, http://bits.blogs.nytimes.com/2009/08/19/study-finds-that-online-education-beats-the-classroom/?emc=eta1

5. For instance, Coburg Senior High School in Melbourne, Victoria, Australia, does not have a library, though there are some books in the school. All students are connected to the Internet, and there are community resources, as Principal Don Collins suggests that the resources outside the school are far more vast than the number of resources he could gather within the school. "Since opening in 2007,

Coburg has become a model of technology revolutionising teaching methods. Computers are integral to everything, with applications ranging from iMovie to FileMaker used across all subjects. Each student has a laptop and work is done online and collaboratively. The environment is closer to that of a university than a traditional high school. The 230 students work in open spaces. There are no formal classrooms, no rows of desks or whiteboards.' We are not anti-pen and paper, it's the context of the program,' Mr Collins says. He says the lack of a library disturbed some librarians. "The reason that we don't have a library is because the whole school is a library. It makes no sense with today's technology," he says, "for students to leave a place of learning and relocate somewhere else where all the information resides." See "Digital Turns a Different Page," by Elizabeth Tarica, *The Age,* Melbourne, August 9, 2010.

6. *Growing Up Digital: The Rise of the Net Generation,* by Donald Tapscott, McGraw-Hill, New York, 1998, page 36.

7. For example, Sharon Summer reports, "I had two 4th grade boys who would go home at night and play with Microsoft Word just so they could come back the next day and show what they had learned. Well, wouldn't you know....this is how I learned that you could insert a picture into WordArt. This was pretty cool. I later did a workshop on Word. One of the student's mothers was in the workshop, so I had him come teach this cool trick. Students teaching the teacher worked then and many, many times through the years. Never hesitate to have the students help you learn about technology! They love helping and will love teaching you!" Sharon Summer, Missouri Baptist University, St. Louis, *Advanced Teaching Online course,* August 23, 2010.

8. *Using Learning Contracts: Practical Approaches to Individualizing and Structuring Learning,* by Malcolm Knowles, Jossey-Bass Publishers, San Francisco, 1986.

9. See "In Education, Furniture Matters Too," by Susan Saulny, *The New York Times,* February 24, 2009, http://www.nytimes.com/2009/02/25/us/25desks.html?src=linkedin.

For more on learning mediums, see *Energizing the Learning Environment,* by William A. Draves, Learning Resources Network, River Falls, WI, 1994.

Finland, the country with the highest test scores, does one thing differently than the schools in other countries, says Ron Clark, author of the education book "The Essential 55." He says students in Finland's schools have 45 minutes of valuable classroom experience, and then 15 minutes of physical exercise or recess every hour of the school day. Source: Ron Clark, keynote address, Institute for Credentialing Excellence, Atlanta, November 17, 2010.

10. "We Have to Operate, But Let's Play First," by Michel Marriott, *The New York Times,* February 24, 2005.

11. "Take off for virtual prototypes," by David Reid, *BBC Online,* September 23, 2005, http://news.bbc.co.uk/2/hi/programmes/click_online/4275332.stm

12. From "Digital habitats and communities of practice: a social discipline of learning," Etienne Wenger, keynote, 26th Annual Distance Learning and Teaching Conference, Madison, Wisconsin, August 6, 2010.

13. Landon Divers interview with the authors, Madison, Wisconsin, 2004.

14. Wenger.

15. "For Today's Graduate, Just One Word: Statistics," by Steve Lohr, *The New York Times,* August 6, 2009.

16. Ibid.

17. See "How good is your child's teacher?" by Jason Felch, *Los Angeles Times,* August 14, 2010.

18. "The Bell Curve," by Atul Gawande, *The New Yorker,* December 6, 2004.

19. "Learning in Stages, Not Ages," *BBC Online,* October 15, 2004, http://news.bbc.co.uk/2/hi/uk_news/education/3747434.stm

20. *Play in Education,* by Joseph Lee, Macmillan Company, New York, 1920. Quotes from page 492, and from pages vii-viii.

21. G. Stanley Hall, in *The Home Teacher, The Chautauqua Industrial Art Desk,* Lewis E. Myers and Company, 1903, page 120.

22. The HighScope Preschool Curriculum Comparison Study found that children who learned mainly through playful activities fared much better at their work and social responsibilities than those in an academic instruction-oriented class. See comments in the August 3, 2010, issue of *The New York Times* by Edward Miller, senior researcher for Alliance for Childhood and co-author of its 2009 report, "Crisis in the Kindergarten: Why Children Need to Play in School."

Separately, a BBC story noted that play is a serious business - and a lack of play opportunities for children is becoming a form of deprivation. See "Generation of Play Deprivation," By Sean Coughlan, Education reporter, *BBC News* http://news.bbc.co.uk/2/hi/uk_news/education/7007378.stm

23."Failure not an option: Ontario students can try, try again," by Joanne Laucius, *Canwest News Service,* May 11, 2009.

24. The concept was first introduced to American educators by Diana Laurillard, Professor of Educational Technology at the Open University, who was then in the Department of Education and Skills, United Kingdom, keynote address at Distance Learning and Teaching, University of Wisconsin, Madison, August 2001. The concept of "personalisation" was adopted as a goal by the Department of Education and Skills.

Chapter 6.
Grading and Assessment: Tests Every Week

1. Several references were consulted regarding the *Academic and Industrial Efficiency Bulletin Number Five,* Morris Llewellyn Cooke, including http://www.carnegiefoundation.org/about-us/foundation-history; http://en.wikipedia.org/wiki/Carnegie_Unit_and_Student_Hour; andhttp://www.suny.edu/facultysenate/TheCarnegieUnit.

2. For example, Douglas Ward, a North Carolina teacher, refused to give standardized tests to his mentally deficient students who would only flunk and feel a sense of failure. Ward refused to administer the tests even though he knew he would be fired and would probably never work as a teacher for the rest of his life. "Basically, the way it was set up, my kids have no chance of passing," said Ward, who has been teaching for three years. "If you have a kid that is 11 years old and only developed to the level of a 1-year-old — I think I am a decent teacher, but I am not good enough to develop him to pass the test." See "Teacher refuses to give N.C. End-of-Grade Tests," by Ashley Wilson, *Citizen-Times,* May 14, 2008.

A Seattle teacher is spending two weeks on leave without pay for refusing to give the Washington Assessment of Student Learning (WASL) to his sixth-graders this month at Eckstein Middle School. "I did it because I think it's bad for kids," Carl Chew, age 60, said. See http://seattletimes.nwsource.com/html/education/2004364815_wasl22m.html.

3. *Gender and Fair Assessment,* by Warren Willingham and Nancy S. Cole, Educational Testing Service, 1997.

4. Commission on the International Learning Unit, www.learningunit.org.

5. For example, United Kingdom educators are advocating more short tests. In a *BBC Online* article, Dr. Ken Boston, the head of UK's testing watchdog agency noted, "But personalised learning, more short tests and training for teachers could get performance moving sharply upwards." See "Test Chief Targets 90% Attainment," *BBC Online,* December 17, 2007, http://news.bbc.co.uk/2/hi/uk_news/education/7148861.stm.

6. "Testing in the 21st Century," William A. Draves keynote, Association of Test Publishers annual conference, March 5, 2008, Dallas, Texas.

7. From "Are School Tests on the Way Out?" by Mike Baker, Education Editor, *BBC Online,* March 24, 2007, http://news.bbc.co.uk/2/hi/uk_news/education/6486767.stm?ls.

Chapter 7.
Grading Learning, not Behavior: No Penalty for Late Work

1. Degrees conferred by institutions of higher education, by level of degree and sex of student, 1949-50 to 1993-94, National Center for Education Statistics, Earned Degrees Conferred.

2. US Department of Homeland Security, H1-B visa statistics, 2007, in "Why There is a Scientist Shortage," http://www.ScientistShortage.com.

3. *USA Today,* February 29, 2008.

4. "The High School Transcript Study," US Department of Education, 2004, page 3-7.

5. Nine Shift: Work, life and education in the 21st century, by William A. Draves and Julie Coates, Learning Resources Network (LERN), 2004.

6. Toronto School Board District, April 16, 2008, http://www.tdsb.on.ca/about_us/media_room/room.asp?show=allNews&view=detailed&self=11565

7. "Using Grades to Assess Student Performance," John Woodward, University of Illinois, in *Journal of School Improvement,* Vol 2, No. 1, Spring. 2001.http://www.ncacasi.org/jsi/2001v2i1/using_grades.

8. *Gender and Fair Assessment,* Warren W. Willingham and Nancy S. Cole, Educational Testing Service, Lawrence Erlbaum Associates, Publishers, New Jersey, 1997.

9. *Gender Difference and Student Learning,* Report to Edina Board of Education, April 2002, Yi Du, Ph.D, Director of Research and Evaluation. http://www.edina.k12.mn.us/news/reports/GenderReport.pdf.

10. "Does Homework Improve Academic Achievement?: A Synthesis of Research," 1987-2003, Harris Cooper, Jorgianne Civey Robinson and Erika A. Patall, Duke University, Review of Educational Research, 2006.

11. A literature search found only one reference to the difference between work turned in on time, and that citation said that girls were equal to boys in work timeliness. Interviews were also conducted by the authors with executives of an Illinois human resources association and a Wisconsin human resources association. Both executives knew of no gender related problem in the workplace with boys. According to the owner and founder of a national employment agency and *Kelly Girl* temporary help, John Willetts of Fox Point, Wisconsin, over the course of several decades of observing young men and young women in the workplace, he cites no significant difference between the punctuality and on-time performance between young men and young women.

Here's more evidence that "teaching responsibility" does not work. There is significant evidence that boys, deemed irresponsible in school, are just as responsible in the workplace. Now Julie has discovered research that girls, deemed responsible in school, are actually "irresponsible" in the workplace in terms of absenteeism, dealing another factual blow that "teaching responsibility" and grading based on behavior has any positive effect. The evidence discovered by Julie is from the Bureau of Labor Standards, Department of Labor, under the leadership of Secretary Hilda Solis. The 2010 government study showed that women are 2-3 times more absent in the workplace than men. This discounts (takes into account) time spent on child care, health issues, and family. So even after subtracting absences due to health, child care and family, women are still 2-3 times more absent in the workplace than men. The study can be found at http://ftp.bls.gov/pub/special.requests/lf/aat46.txt

Julie reports that two previous studies also reach the same conclusion, the earliest of which was done around 1990. All studies indicate that women perform at the same level as men in the workplace, just like boys perform academically at the same level as girls in school. For our purposes, what these workplace gender studies demonstrate is that faculty are not "teaching responsibility" and that grading based on behavior has no positive impact for either male or female students.

12. Interviews with faculty who do not penalize students for turning in homework late indicate there are no problems with the policy. Sissy Copeland of Piedmont Technical College has had this policy for several years without any problems. Bruce Jones of West Georgia College reported only one student out of 43 had academic problems with the no-penalty for late homework policy. Carol Ann Baily of

Middle Tennessee State University provides bonus points for homework turned in on time, but does not penalize a student for late work. Robert O. Phillips of Eastern New Mexico University reports that students turn in homework in the same time pattern when there is no penalty as when there were late penalties. That is, most students turned in homework on time even when there was no penalty for late work.

13. United States Congress, House Committee on the Judiciary, March 28, 1924. Child Labor, compiled by Julia E. Johnsen, HW Wilson Company, New York, 1924, page 145.

Chapter 8.
The Pedagogy of Trains: How Trains Change Education

1. "Real-estate markets that have been less affected or quicker to recover include Boston and San Francisco, which have strong urban rail systems. In New Jersey, Connecticut, Boston, Denver and Chicago, housing prices near new or existing train stations have either been among the first to recover or have seen less depreciation during the bursting of the housing bubble." From "Is Digital Revolution Driving Decline in U.S. Car Culture?" by Jack Neff, Editor at Large, *Advertising Age,* May 31, 2010.

2. National Association for Pupil Transportation, napt.org.

3. *Kiplinger Letter* Associate Editor Jim Ostroff reports, "The federal government's coming transportation legislation will favor cities and states that adopt zoning policies aimed at reducing traffic congestion -- a philosophical shift that will bring about the most significant land use changes since the creation of the interstate highway system. The new mindset seeks to reverse past planners' "build it and they will come" mentality -- the kind of thinking that led to urban sprawl and helped create a heavy reliance on motor vehicles for getting around. States and cities will have to rethink zoning to permit more mixed-use projects, including those that combine residential, retail and commercial developments, which for decades have been largely segregated, requiring Americans to hop into their cars to go to work, stores, playgrounds, etc." *Highway Bill to Spur Land Use Changes,* by Jim Ostroff, Associate Editor, *Kiplinger Letter,* May 24, 2010.

4. Richard Louv, author of *Last Child in the Woods: Saving Our Children From Nature-Deficit Disorder,* in Wisconsin Public Radio interview, March 20, 2009.

5. The National Household Transportation Survey of 2009, Department of Transportation, shows a 15-year decline in miles driven by young people. In 2009, driving was down 37% for young people as compared to 1995. The decline was first noted in the DOT's 2001 report data, then accelerated by 2009. At the same time, the percentage of people in Gen Y with driver's licenses declined. And a Pew Research poll shows that Gen Y values cars much less than older generations. Projecting out, especially with telework continuing to grow and more passenger train service being built, we estimate driving in 2020 will be half of what it is in 2010, marking the end of the era of the automobile as the primary transportation mode in the United States, and the beginning of light rail and trains as the primary transportation mode for those age 40 and under in 2020.

Chapter 9.
Financing: Building 21st Century Schools and Colleges

1.Some education leaders already recognize the need to produce more graduates. For example, the University of Wisconsin-Madison announced in 2010 a plan to pay for supporting more than 5,900 additional undergraduates over a two-year span. The additional students include more than 2,200 that the system would normally have expected to have dropped out between their freshman and sophomore years of college. The cost is less than $2,000 per student to produce an additional 30% graduates. See "Price tag for UW plan to issue more degrees: $22.6 million," by Sharif Durhams and Rick Romell, *The Milwaukee Journal Sentinel,* August 16, 2010.

Tuition can be reduced substantially without negatively impacting academic quality. For instance, at the University of Tulsa, continuing education dean Paula Hogard was able to cut credit tuition by 25% for continuing education students. The tuition was reduced because continuing education students, usually working adults, did not utilize the university's non-academic services which the traditional 18-22 year old campus based students used, such as dormitories, cafeteria, student union, gymnasium, sports and other non-academic services. The University of Tulsa is a private university, so does not receive tax payer funding and is necessarily financially self-sufficient, and Hogard reported to the authors that the university was still able to cover its costs with the 25% reduction in tuition for continuing education students. Source: Conversation with the authors, September 30, 2010.

2. "The Physical Plant: Asset or Liability?" by William A. Daigneau, in *ASHE Reader on Finance in Higher Education,* Second Edition, James L. Ratcliff, Series Editor, Pearson Custom Publishing, Boston, 2001, page 372.

3. "College and University Budgeting: What Do We Know? What Do We Need to Know?" William F. Lasher and Deborah L. Greene, in *The Finance of Higher Education: Theory, Research, Policy and Practice,* Edited by Michael B. Paulsen and John C. Smart, Agathon Press, New York, 2001, page 503.

4. Robert K. Toutkoushian, "Trends in Revenues and Expenditures for public and private higher education," Robert K. Toutkoushian, in *The Finance of Higher Education: Theory, Research, Policy and Practice,* Edited by Michael B. Paulsen and John C. Smart, Agathon Press, New York, 2001, pg 25.

5. "Rising Administrative Costs," by Larry L. Leslie and Gary Rhoades, in *ASHE Reader on Finance in Higher Education,* page 337.

6. "The Costs of Failure Factories in American Higher Education," American Enterprise Institute for Public Policy Research, Mark Schneider, October 2008.

7. Ibid.

8. Student View, Victorian Government, Australia, in Moreland Leader, November 9, 2009. Begun in 2007 with Don Collins as Principal, the model for Coburg Senior High School in Victoria, Australia, has received worldwide attention and recognition for its innovation and effectiveness.

Chapter 10.
The Neurology of Learning

1. *Descartes' Error: Emotion, Reason and the Human Brain,* by Antonio Demasio, New York: G. P. Putnam's Sons, 1994.

2. *Making Connections: Teaching and the Human Brain,* by Renate Numella Caine and Geoffrey Caine, Addision-Wesley, 1994.

3. Demasio.

4. *Brain Based Learning,* by Jeb P. Schenck, Wyoming Community Education Association Conference, Jackson, WY, 2005.

5. *Teaching With the Brain in Mind,* by Eric Jensen, Alexandria, VA: Association for Supervision and Curriculum Development, 2005.

6. "Implementing and Supporting Hybrid Online Learning in a K-12 Environment," C.J. Lovejoy and Victoria Jaeger, 26th Annual Conference on Distance Teaching and Learning. Madison, WI, 2010.

Chapter 11.
Inside the Male and Female Brain

1. *The Trend of the Teens,* by M.V. O'Shea, Chicago: Frederick J. Drake & Co., 1920.

2. *Digest of Education Statistics, Center for Education Statistics,* Washington, DC: U. S. Department of Education, 2007.

3. *The Dragons of Eden,* by Carl Sagan, Ballentine Books, New York, 1977.

4. *Boys and Girls Learn Differently,* by Michael Gurian, San Francisco: Jossey Bass, 2001.

5. *BBC Science and Nature.* Retrieved September 22, 2010, from BBC : http://www.bbc.co.uk/science/humanbody/sex/add_user.shtml.

6. Ibid.

7. *The Essential Difference: Men, Women and the Extreme Male Brain,* by Simon Baron-Cohen, London: Penguin Books, 2004.

8. *What Could He be Thinking?: How a Man's Mind Really Works,* by Michael Gurian, New York: St. Martin's Press, 2003.

9. Gurian, 2001.

10. *Reclaiming Kindergarten: Making Kindergarten Less Harmful to Boys,* by Leonard Sax, *Psychology of Men and Masculinity* Vol. 2, No. I,, 3-12, 2001.

11. Ibid.

12. Gurian, 2001.

13. Sax.

14. *Girls Have Big Advantage Over Boys on Timed Tests.* Kennedy Research Center for Human Development, Vanderbilt University, 2006.

15. Ibid. Additional references:
   Hall, J. A. (1978). "Gender Effects in Decoding Nonverbal Cues." *Psychological Bulletin, v85 n4,* p845-57.
   Mehrabian, A. (1971). *Silent Messages.* Belmont: Wadsworth Publishing Co.
   Svoboda..., B. J. (2000). *Mensight Magazine.* Retrieved 06 23, 2008, from http://mensightmagazine.com/reviews/Svoboda/boysandgirls. htm

Chapter 12.
Helping Males to Succeed

1. U.S. Department of Education, Institute of Education Sciences, National Center for Education Statistics, High School Transcript Study (HSTS), 2000.

2. Office of the Vice President for Academic Affairs, Truman State University, Missouri. Truman GPA by gender for freshman, sophomore, junior and senior classes for 1999-2000, 2000-2001, and 2001-2002 reprinted in *Smart Boys Bad Grades,* by Julie Coates and William Draves, LERN, 2006.

3. "The Gender Gap in College Expections" by John Reynolds, Florida State University quoting *Monitoring the Future Survey.* Chart of High School Seniors' Educational Expectations by Gender, 1976-1999, reprinted in *Smart Boys Bad Grades,* by Julie Coates and William Draves, page 19.

4. *Gender and Fair Assessment,* Warren W. Willingham and Nancy S. Cole, Educational Testing Service, Lawrence Erlbaum Associates, Publishers, New Jersey, 1997, page 57.

5. American College Testing (ACT), http://www.act.org/news/releases/2004/8-18-04.html.

6. "Gender and High School GPA, An Example of Correlational Research," Alan E. Marks, Department of Psychology, Oglethorpe University, 2004, www.oglethorpe.edu/faculty/.

7. University of Massachusetts, Amherst, "SAT Scores (Recentered) and High School Grade Point Average for Entering First-Year Students by Gender, Fall 1993 – Fall 2004."

8. *Boys and Girls Learn Differently!* by Michael Gurian, Jossey Bass Publishers, San Francisco, 2001, page 45.

9. Laura Burkey, http://www.positivepath.net/ideasLB3.asp.

10. *Self Direction for Lifelong Learning,* by Philip C. Candy, Jossey Bass Publishers, San Francisco, 1991, page 391.

11. *Advanced Teaching Online,* by William A. Draves, LERN, Second Edition, 2007, page 133.

12. Ibid, page 136.

13. Study of Carleton College Alumni comments from 2004 reunion book for the Class of 1971.

14. "We Have to Operate, but Let's Play First," by Michel Marriott, *New York Times,* February 24, 2005.

15. Willingham and Cole.

16. "Gender Difference and Student Learning," Report to Edina Board of Education, April 2002, Yi Du, Ph.D, Director of Research and Evaluation. http://www.edina.k12.mn.us/news/reports/GenderReport.pdf.

17. "Gender differences in approaches to studying for the GCSE among high achieving pupils," Lynne Rogers, Open University, and Sue Hallam, University of London, in *Educational Studies,* Vol. 32, No. 1, March 2006, pages 59-71.

18. "Gender and Homework Management Reported by High School Students," Xu, Jianzhong, Educational Psychology, Volume 26, Number 1, February 2006, pp. 73-91.

19. Rogers and Hallam.

20. Jianzhong Xu.

21. Roger Highfield and Paul Carter, "The Private Lives of Albert Einstein," NY: St. Martin's Press, 1993.

22. The Sexual Paradox, by Susan Pinker, Scribner, New York, 2008, page 34.

23. Interview with Coates and Draves, Orlando, Florida, 2002.

24. Interview with William A. Draves, 2005.

25. Draves and Coates, *Nine Shift,* page 210.

26. Ibid, Page 213.

27. Ibid, pages 213 – 214.

Chapter 13.
Helping Female Students Learn More

1. *The Sexual Paradox,* by Susan Pinker, Scribner, New York, 2008, page 149.

2. Cit 16 Statistics Canada, "The Gap in Achievement between Boys and Girls," March 9, 2006, www.statcan.ca/english/freepub/81-004-XIE/200410/male.htm.

3. Pinker, page 118.

4. Simon Baron-Cohen, "Sex Differences in Mind: Keeping Science Distinct from Social Policy;" quoted in Pinker, page 199.

5. *New Girl on the Job,* by Hannah Seligson, page 158.

6. Ibid, page 160.

7. College instructor from LaCrosse, Wisconsin on Wisconsin Public Radio, May, 2009.

8. "A Call for K–16 Engineering Education," by Jacquelyn F. Sullivan, The Bridge, Volume 36, Number 2 - Summer 2006.

9. New Earnings Survey Data Set, 2001, Department for Skills and Education, United Kingdom.

10. Pinker, pages 64-65.

11. Data on H1-B visa entrants to the United States provided to Draves by Commerce Department, United States Government.

12. "Structural differences/choices," *MIT Technology Review,* Jan/Feb 2008.

13. *Sex and Cognition,* by Doreen Kimura, page 122.

14. Data researched by Julie Coates for faculty development seminar

for the School of Engineering, University of Kansas, January 19, 2009, Lawrence, Kansas.

15. "Long-Term Effects of a Middle School Engineering Outreach Program for Girls: A Controlled Study," by Jeanne Hubelbank, WPI Evaluation Consulting, AC 2007-1106.

Chapter 14.
Students with Asperger's and Autism

This chapter was originally written by Julie Coates on the request of Dr. Christopher Babbit, psychologist, as a briefing for school officials in the state of Minnesota. Julie is the parent of a son with Aspberger Syndrome. She recommends the following book as a reference.

Asperger Syndrome and Adolescence: Practical Solutions for School Success, by Brenda Smith Myles and Diane Adreon, Autism Asperger Publishing Company, Shawnee Mission, Kansas, 2001, ISBN 0-9672514-9-4.

About the Authors

Coates and Draves are two of education's leading futurists and co-authors of *Nine Shift: Work, life and education in the 21st Century.* The BBC calls *Nine Shift* "Fascinating." The American Institute of Architects wrote, "Not since John Naisbitt's Megatrends has a book hit the mark so clearly."

They are the most frequently quoted experts in lifelong learning by the U.S. media, having appeared on the BBC, NPR, CBS radio, NBC TV and interviewed by The New York Times, Wall Street Journal, Newsweek, Associated Press and many more.

They teach K-12 teachers and higher education faculty and have mentored low income African American boys.

Julie Coates is author of the pioneering book, *Generational Learning Styles,* and one of the foremost authorities on gender and learning. She has given presentations all over the United States, including Harvard, and in Russia, the United Kingdom, Australia, Germany and Mexico.

She serves as Vice President for Information Services at LERN, and also teaches in the graduate program in Adult and Higher Education for the University of South Dakota.

Julie was born and raised in Black Mountain, North Carolina. She attended Cornell University, North Carolina State University, and pursued graduate study in public administration and adult education at Kansas State University, from which she earned her Master's Degree.

As a leader in the civil rights movement in North Carolina in the 1960s, she was a target of the Klu Klux Klan, and also worked in the war on poverty. She has taught in an elementary school, ran one of the nation's premiere lifelong learning programs, and initiated such community development programs as the statewide folk life program for Kansas, a day-care center, avocational programs for adults with disabilities and community-wide volunteer clearinghouse.

221

William A. Draves is an author, consultant, teacher and President of the Learning Resources Network. He has authored six other books on education, does consulting for education institutions, conducts faculty development seminars, and has taught more than 6,000 faculty and K-12 teachers about teaching online.

Bill was born and raised in Fond du Lac, Wisconsin, attended Carleton College and the University of Wisconsin at Madison, and holds a Master's Degree in adult education from The George Washington University in Washington, DC.

He has done speaking engagements throughout the world, for business, associations, and in education for Superintendents of Education, K-12 teachers, faculty in higher education, community college and university administrators, and for educational associations such as the Alabama Association of School Boards and the Association of Test Publishers. Maureen Geddes, vice president of the Ontario Speakers Association calls him "a world class speaker" and educator Phil Housel of Kerrville, Texas, says, "I'd trample my grandma to hear Draves speak."

Other Books by Julie Coates and William A. Draves

By William A. Draves and Julie Coates
Nine Shift: Work, life and education in the 21st Century

By Julie Coates
Generational Learning Styles

By William A. Draves
Advanced Teaching Online
How to Teach Adults
Energizing the Learning Environment

About LERN

The Learning Resources Network (LERN) is a nonprofit international education association with 5,000 members in over 1,000 organizations in the United States, Canada and several other countries.

LERN specializes in practical, how-to information. Areas of specialty include faculty development, online teaching, and continuing education. We are the leading information and consulting organization in the world in the field of continuing education.

LERN works with faculty and staff in a variety of institutional settings, including universities, community colleges, public schools, recreation departments, associations, and other nonprofit organizations.

Services include consulting, publications, seminars, online courses, training, software, conferences, research and more. Areas of expertise include teaching, learning, marketing, programming, finance and budgeting, market research, needs assessment, faculty development, online teaching, pricing, and more.

Some of the certifications LERN provides include the Certified Online Instructor (COI), Certified Faculty Developer (CFD) and Certified Program Planner (CPP) designations. We have partnered with the University of South Dakota to offer a graduate degree in adult and higher education.

LERN has a staff of around 20 people. In 1998 we became a virtual organization, with staff and consultants now working in at least eight states and two countries. Founded in 1974, LERN is governed by a Board of Directors.

For more, visit our web site at lern.org or contact our staff.

Share Pedagogy 21
With your colleagues

Name
_____

Title or Department (if any)
_____

Organization
_____

Address
_____

City,   State/Province,   Zip/Postal Code

Email address   Phone #

Please check one:
____ One copy, $20 plus $6 shipping = $26 total
____ Ten copies, $99 plus $10 shipping = $109 total
For other quantities, send email to info@lern.org.

Please check one:
____ Payment enclosed
____ Charge my credit card

For overnight shipping or more information, call LERN at 800-678-5376 or send email to *info@lern.org*

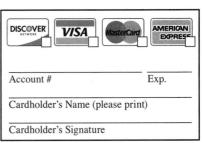

Account #   Exp.

Cardholder's Name (please print)

Cardholder's Signature

To Order The Pedagogy of the 21st Century
Call: 800-678-5376 (US and Canada)
Fax, toll free: 888-234-8633 (toll free worldwide)
Email: info@lern.org
Web: www.Pedagogy21.com or www.lern.org
Mail to: LERN Books, P.O. Box 9, River Falls, WI 54022 USA